THE *WRITE* WAY TO POSITIVE PARENTING

THE *WRITE* WAY TO POSITIVE PARENTING

By

EDITH NAMM, M.A., C.S.G.
Certified Specialized Handwriting Analyst

1st Books -- rev.5/11/00

ABOUT THE BOOK

THE WRITE WAY TO POSITIVE PARENTING

A Resource Manual that shows and tells, in a simplified capsule form, what it takes for you as a Parent to empower yourself and your Child to feel Confident, experience a Sense of Well Being, successfully cope with the stress of Daily Living, and have a healthy, satisfying, productive life.

The Manual takes you on an exciting journey to discover

How to recognize the signs of Emotional Stress - Anger, Resentment,Fear, and Depression - in One's Behavior and Handwriting.

The impact of Emotional Stress on all Body Systems.

The Write Way to handle Emotional Stress.

The Winning Ways to boost the Immune System.

The Write Way to a Positively Energized Self Image and Belief System.

The Write Way to learn the 8 significant Letter Shapes that show and tell that a Writer is a Confident, Effective Communicator.

The Basics for Effective Communication and Satisfying Parent/Child Relationships.

The ABC'S for creating a Safe, Nurturing Home Environment.

The Basic Concepts of Handwriting Analysis in Simple Capsule Form

20 Tips On How To Feel Good About Yourself - *A Manual for Pre-Teens and Adolescents*

Dear Parent,

Upon my retirement as a Guidance Counselor with the New York City Board of Education, I chose to seriously pursue a long time interest – Graphology, The Science of Handwriting Analysis. Within 2 years of intensive study, I became a Certified Specialized Handwriting Analyst.

This has been a truly exciting and significant experience. I discovered the "Write Way" for an Individual to have a Positive Self Image and experience Joy and Peace of Mind -- the essential ingredients for a Healthy, Productive Satisfying Life !!!

I discovered the "Write Way" to accurately and objectively evaluate a Child's Emotional Growth and Energy Level!!! I discovered the "Write Way" to recognize the signs of Emotional Stress in a Child's Handwriting!!!

I felt compelled to share my discoveries with all Parents – regardless of Age, Gender, or Socio-economic Level. To fulfill this commitment, I planned to write a Book.

Based upon intensive research in the field of Behavioral Science, 25 years of experience in the field of Education as a Language Arts Teacher and Guidance Counselor, 10 years of experience as a Certified Specialized Handwriting Analyst, and 40 years of experience as a Parent, the creative phase of my journey gave rise to --

THE WRITE WAY TO POSITIVE PARENTING

A Resource Manual that shows and tells, in a simplified capsule form, what it takes for you as a Parent to empower yourself and your Child to feel Confident, experience a Sense of Well Being, successfully cope with the stress of Daily Living, and have a healthy, satisfying, productive Life.

The Manual takes you on an exciting journey to discover how to recognize the signs of Emotional Stress, Anger, Resentment, Fear, and Depression - in One's Behavior and Handwriting.

The impact of Emotional Stress on all Body Systems. The Write Way to handle Emotional Stress.

The Winning Ways to boost the Immune System.

The Write Way to a Positively Energized Self Image and Belief System.

The Write Way to learn the 8 significant Letter Shapes that show and tell that a Writer is a Confident, Effective Communicator.

The Basics for Effective Communication and Satisfying Parent/Child Relationships.

The ABC'S for creating a Safe, Nurturing Home Environment.

The Basic Concepts of Handwriting Analysis in Simple Capsule Form.

20 Tips On How To Feel Good About Yourself *- A Manual for Pre-Teens and Adolescents.*

Planning and preparing the Road Map for your journey has been an exciting and rewarding experience for me.

I welcome you aboard. Travel at a speed that is comfortable for you. Travel with the confidence of knowing that as a result of your journey, your Child is learning the Winning Ways for Positive Parenting. The way a Child is parented, is the way he/she, in turn, will parent.

CONTENTS

SOME WORDS ABOUT HANDWRITTEN COMMUNICATION FROM A HANDWRITING ANALYST'S POINT OF VIEW

Handwritten Communication is the "write connection" for getting in touch with One's Inner Feelings of Anger, Fear, Sadness, Love, Joy, and Hope.

Every Handwritten Message reveals a Writer's Inner Feeling at the time the writing instrument is applied to paper.

Handwriting is really Brainwriting!!!

Brain Impulses direct all your Activity and Movements.

Learning to write involves your entire Neuro-Muscular System.

The Neuro-Muscular Skill of Handwriting becomes a habit that is stored in your Brain's Memory Data Bank.

When it is time for Written Communication, your Brain accesses the Writing Skill Program from your Memory Data Bank and sends Neuro-Muscular Impulses to your Hand.

Your Hand moves the pen to record the Feelings, Thoughts, and Ideas that your Brain wishes to express.

Your Hand is the Neuro-Muscular Connection between your Brain and the paper !!!

A Child's Handwritten Message can show and tell when a Child is feeling troubled.

A Child's Sense of Security is severely compromised whenever he/she is exposed to traumatic disastrous events. As a result of exposure to disastrous events, a Child experiences Fear and Anxiety. An emotionally stressed Child has difficulty talking about his/her feelings.

A Child cannot feel good about him/her self until he/she lets go of his/her Angry, Sad, Scared Feelings.

A Child learns how to deal with Anger, Fear, Anxiety, and Sadness by observing how his/her Parent deals with Anger, Fear, Anxiety, and Sadness.

Use Handwritten Communication to deal with your Emotional Stress.

Encourage your Child to use Handwritten Communication to deal with his/her Emotional Stress.

Handwritten Communication is the Write Way to heal the emotional pain caused by exposure to traumatic, disastrous events.

Handwritten Communication can empower You and your Child to feel Comfortable, Confident, and Self-filled.

For Your Information:

Newsworthy Item reported in The New York Times on Wednesday, April 14, 1999, concerns a Study published in the April Issue of the Journal of the American Medical Association.

A research study, conducted by Dr. Joshua Smyth at the State University of New York at Stony Brook School of Medicine, demonstrated that patients, suffering from chronic Asthma or Rheumatoid Arthritis, who wrote about their past traumatic experiences, for 20 minutes a day on 3 consecutive days, showed significant, measurable improvement in their health.

Also mentioned in the article -- Work by other researchers show that the writing exercise can boost Immune System functioning and give healthy Individuals a Feeling of Well-Being.

The findings cited in the study dramatically confirms that Emotional Stress can have an impact on an Individual's Body Systems, and that writing exercises can reduce an Individual's Emotional Stress and Physical Tension, and can increase an Individual's Sense of Well- Being.

SOME WORDS ABOUT FEELINGS – THE SOURCE FOR HUMAN EMOTIONAL ENERGY

From A Guidance Counselor's Point of View

Human Beings function and survive on Emotional Energy -- FEELINGS

Feelings influence what You Think.

What You Think influences what You Believe.

What You Believe influences how You Act.

How You Act influences Your Relationships with Others.

Positive and Negative Feelings cannot occupy the same space in the same Body at the same time.

Only one Feeling can be expressed at any one time.

When You feel Love, You do not feel Anger.

When You feel Happy, You do not feel Sad.

When You feel Secure, You do not feel Fear.

When You smile, You do not frown.

When You hug, You do not fight.

When You laugh, You do not cry.

When You compliment, You do not criticize.

When You feel Comfortable, You like the way You feel. The Good Feelings of Joy, Love, and Hope are filling your mind and Body with the Positive Energy that you need in order to feel good about Yourself.

When You feel Uncomfortable, You don't like the way You feel. The painful feelings of Anger, Fear, Sadness, or Depression are causing You to experience Emotional Stress.

Feelings of LOVE, JOY, and HOPE empower You to successfully satisfy your needs, have lifelong loving relationships, and successfully cope with the Stress and Tension of everyday living.

Feelings of ANGER, FEAR, SADNESS, or DEPRESSION deprive You of the power to function effectively.

Human Beings function on the Negative Energy Program or the Positive Energy Program.

When an Individual is under continual Emotional Stress – Feelings of Anger, Fear, Anxiety, Sadness or Depression, he/she is functioning on the Negative Energy Program. He/she suffers from an Unhealthy Negative Belief System, has a Poor Self-image, Low Self Esteem, is unable to maintain Satisfying Social Relationships, and engages in Socially Unacceptable Activities.

When an Individual experiences the pleasurable Feelings of Love, Joy and Hope, he/she is functioning on the Positive energy Program. He/she has a Healthy, Positive Belief System, a Positive Self- Image, High Self-Esteem, Satisfying Social Relationships, and engages in Healthy, Socially Acceptable Activities.

It is essential that the Causes and Consequences of Emotional Stress be addressed and recognized, in order to maximize One's Positive Energy Power, and effectively function on the Positive Energy Program.

RECOGNIZING THE SIGNS OF ANGER

Anger is a natural emotion, that is here to stay, never goes away, and can be experienced by any Individual -- regardless of Age, Gender, or Socio-economic Level, at any time, in any place.

Anger comes in many forms, shapes, sizes, intensities - frustration, hostility, irritability, impatience, jealousy, hate, fury, greed, moodiness, procrastination, resentment, rage.

Anger is a reaction to painful traumatic experiences of abandonment, abuse that can be verbal, emotional, physical, or sexual, betrayal, deprivation, neglect, or rejection.

It is necessary for Feelings of Anger to be identified, released, defused, and appropriately expressed.

If Feelings of Anger are ignored or denied, they will fester and become toxic Repressed Anger.

Why Repressed Anger is hazardous to your Emotional and Physical Well- Being.

It destroys Self- Esteem.

It adversely affects every relationship, by interfering with a person's ability to trust and relate well with others.

It keeps an Individual stuck in the period of time when the painful experience occurred, thus perpetuating pain and tension, and retarding Emotional Growth.

It prevents an Individual from achieving a satisfactory resolution to a problem.

It increases in intensity to explosive levels of Rage and Violence against One's Self and Others.

Repressed Anger in School Age Children

Behavioral Clues

Appears boisterous, rebellious, defiant.

Engages in Self-Destructive, Addictive, Abusive Behavior alcohol, drugs, smoking, eating disorders

Violates the safety of Others.

Disrespects the rights of Others.

Annoys, humiliates, insults, ridicules, teases, threatens Others.

Self Destructive Behavior reflects underlying Feelings of SELF HATE and SELF DOUBT.

"t-bars" and "i-dots" Show and Tell Feelings of Anger

Count the number of "t-bars" in any Handwriting Sample.

TOTAL_____
Tally and total the number of "t-bars"
to the left of the "t-stem"_____Total_____
to the right of the "t-stem"_____Total_____
that are long, strong, balanced, and placed close to the top of the "t-stem"

_____Total_____

What the "t-bars" show and tell

The number of "t-bars" to the left of the "t-stem," in comparison to the total number of "t-bars," shows and tells the degree of Procrastination and Frustration a Writer experienced at the time of writing.

The number of "t-bars" to the right of the "t-stem," in comparison to the total number of "t-bars," shows and tells how much Anger a Writer experienced at the time of writing.

The number of long, strong "t-bars", in comparison to the total number of "t-bars", shows and tells the level of Confidence a Writer experienced at the time of writing.

Count the number of "i" and "j" dots in a Handwriting Sample.

Total_____

Tally and Total the number of "i" and "j" dots that are slashes.

_____Total_____

Tally and Total the number of "i" and "j" dots that are dots placed close to the stem.

_____Total_____

What the "i" and "j" dots show and tell

The number of dot slashes, in comparison to the total number of "i-dots", shows and tells the degree of Irritability and Impatience a Writer experienced at the time of writing.

The number of "i-dots" placed close to the stem, in comparison to the total number of "i-dots", shows and tells how Accurate, and Observant a Writer was at the time of writing.

THE STRESSFUL FEELING OF ANXIETY

Anxiety exists when a situation, based upon the unknown, is viewed to be a threat to One's State of Well Being.

Anxiety is based upon Fear of anticipated pain in the future -- "what ifs" that are to be. An Anxious Person turns specific issues and situations into self-defeating generalizations by exaggerating their meaning, and imagining the worst scenarios.

Why Anxiety is a "no-win" Situation

It is based on inaccurate assumptions, distorted perceptions, misinformation, exaggerations, rumors, gossip, hearsay.

It is impossible to accurately visualize what One does not know or has not experienced. It is impossible to predict what is ahead until One gets there.

"if only" statements have no accurate conclusions. "what if's" are a futile attempt to control an unpredictable situation.

It has a paralyzing effect on One's ability to positively function. It makes One shiver and shake regardless of weather conditions.

ZEROING IN ON THE FEELING OF SADNESS

Sadness is a result of experiencing a Loss.

Loss of a person's love through traumatic circumstances - death, divorce, illness, violence

Loss of possessions because of catastrophic disasters beyond one's control

Each Individual has his/her own time frame for expressing grief.

Each Individual has his/her own way of expressing grief.

There is no right or wrong way to grieve.

There are stages within the Grieving Process.

It is important for each Individual to work through each phase in order to complete the Grieving Process.

An Individual who gets stuck in any one phase, remains with a sad, angry, fearful memory.

The Process of Grieving is a learning experience -- learning new ways to live through Loss and Disappointment.

Phases of the Grieving Process

Denial
Feelings of shock, disbelief, and helplessness

Anger
Having to face the reality of the loss

Bargaining
Seeking explanations, rationalizing, attempting to undo the loss.

Depression
Sadness over the loss.

Acceptance

Willingness to confront the loss.

Willingness to accept the fact that life is different and that it is time to move on.

Grieving Individuals need support PLUS CARE.

P L U S -- Patience, Love, Understanding, Security

C A R E -- Comfort, Attention, Reassurance, Encouragement

THE MANY SIDES AND SIGNS OF DEPRESSION

Depression

A reaction to an upsetting event or loss.

An Individual's inability to accept what is.

An Individual's inability to appropriately express painful feelings.

Can affect any Individual regardless of age, gender, or socio-economic level.

Can have varying degrees of intensity and duration.

-- mild, moderate, severe, transitory, persistent

A Depressed Person feels hopeless, helpless, and worthless and engages in self-destructive, risk taking, abusive behavior.

Causes

A change in family structure - divorce, death, illness.

A loss of someone or something that has been loved.

Deprivation of love in childhood.

Chemical changes within the Body.

Post Partum Depression- experienced by a Mother, 2 - 6 weeks after Childbirth

Causes

Emotional Stress - Fear of Failure in the new parental role.

Physical Bio-Chemical Imbalance - hormonal and metabolic adjustments take place when a woman goes from the pregnant state to the non-pregnant state. It can take as long as a year for the Body to heal, recover, and restore the Bio- chemical Balance.

Sleep Deprivation.

Drastic change in lifestyle.

Lack of parenting skills.

A Depressed Mother
Experiences frustration, disappointment, and fatigue.

She is physically and emotionally unable to meet a baby's basic nurturing needs for love, security, and safety.

She is unable to provide a positive bonding relationship with the baby.

Consequences of a Mother's Inability to Provide a Positive Bonding Relationship With Her Baby
The Baby is deprived of adequate emotional stimulation.

The Baby becomes depressed when he/she misses a loving Mother.

The Baby suffers its first significant experience in Loss of Love.

The primary negative bonding experience interferes with the Child's ability to form positive relationships in later years.

Behaviorial Clues of Infant Depression
Baby is unresponsive, lethargic, and constantly crying.

Baby is not eating or sleeping well and is slow to gain weight, sit or crawl.

Baby pays little attention to the immediate surroundings.

Baby rarely smiles.

Resource for available help, printed material and information about support groups.

Depression after Delivery
P.O. Box 1282
Morrisville, Pa. 19067
215-295-3994

Childhood and Teenage Depression
Retards a Child's Positive Emotional Growth
and Development.
Negatively affects a Child's Personal
and Social Relationships.
Interferes with a Child's ability to function effectively.

Masked Depression in Pre-Schoolers
Behavioral Clues
Child is unable to verbalize his/her concerns and fears.

Child appears to be aggressive, irritable, cranky.

Child has temper tantrums.

Child has difficulty following rules and making friends.

Child either has difficulty sitting still or withdraws to a corner.

Child seeks isolation and avoids group situations.

Child has disturbed sleep patterns, and nightmares.

Masked Depression in School Age Children
Behavioral Clues
Child appears to be moody, indifferent, listless, rebellious, aggressive, defiant.

Child has difficulty concentrating.

Child has poor sleeping and eating habits.

Child has unexplained physical symptoms of headaches, stomachaches, vague aches and pains.

Child has a loss of interest in activities previously enjoyed.

Causes
Family conflicts and tension.

Parental neglect or abuse - physical, verbal, emotional, or sexual.

Love deprivation.

Severe loss or separation from a meaningful relationship with persons or pets, divorce, death.

Chronic illness.

Peer rejection.

Environmental changes in home or at school.

Masked Depression in Teenagers
Behavioral Clues
Acts tough, boisterous, rebellious, irrational, impulsive, defiant, hyperactive.

Acts indifferent to surroundings, environment, people, events.

Has a short attention span and inability to concentrate.

Has disturbed sleep patterns.

Is accident prone.

Is pre-occupied with thoughts of death.

Engages in self-destructive, risk taking, abusive behavior such as alcohol, drugs, smoking, eating disorders, obsessive compulsions, reckless driving, promiscuity.

Childhood Depression Can Lead To Suicide.
Suicide is

A cry for help to be noticed.

An attempt to end the pain of Depression.

A self-destructive message that may be verbal or written.

Causes
A sudden loss of an important relationship.

Fear of Rejection.

Fear of Failure -- inability to live up to parent's unrealistic expectations.

Self-Hate, Self-Doubt, Low Self-Esteem.

Behavioral Clues
Inability to cope with the routine tasks of daily living.

Withdrawal from family, friends, and activities.

Giving away favorite possessions.

Increased use of drugs and /or alcohol.

Inability to concentrate, confused irrational thinking.

Academic failure.

Loss of appetite.

Sleep disturbances.

Not goal oriented.

ALL SUICIDE THREATS - EXPRESSED VERBALLY OR IN WRITING -- MUST BE TAKEN SERIOUSLY!!!

Suicide Threats are not to be denied, belittled or minimized.

If you fear that someone is suicidal, never leave that person alone.

Seek immediate professional help. Contact a Crisis Center.

Parents and Teachers must learn to recognize the Emotional, Behavioral, and Graphic Signs of Depression and Suicide.

Parents and Teachers must frequently review a Child's handwriting sample to note any significant negative changes that may reflect the presence of Depression.

Grapho-Indicators can show and tell Depression or Suicidal Intent.

A combination of Indicators must be present to have an accurate assessment of Depression.

Extremes and inconsistencies in Slant, Pressure, Letter Size.

Illegible, tangled script.

Descending, erratic Baseline - words or word endings that droop below the Baseline.

Weak, poorly formed "t-bars"

Distorted letter formations.

Note:

Suicidal people usually kill themselves on impulse.

A Suicidal Baseline may involve only a few lines or words on a page of writing.

A descent may suddenly appear in the last word or words, or last letters of a word at the end of a line at the right margin.

Studies have indicated that people who had successfully committed Suicide, tended to write short Suicide notes.

Those who were unsuccessful in their Suicide attempts, wrote long notes and managed to be saved in time.

CHILDHOOD FEARS

Physical Safety and Emotional Security are basic needs for every Human Being.

Fear is Emotional Insecurity. Negative messages, and traumatic experiences threaten a Child's Sense of Security. A Child responds with Fear to what he/she feels and believes to be unsafe events, actions, or experiences.

It is the responsibility of Primary Caregivers to recognize
-    the existence of Fear and Anxiety in a Child.
-    the negative messages and experiences that generate Fear and Anxiety.
-    the supportive measures needed to help a Child appropriately deal with his/her Fears.

Recognizing Childhood Fears

Fear of Ridicule - Self-Consciousness
The Child feels inadequate, unaccepted, unworthy, inferior to others, and is uncomfortable in unfamiliar surroundings.

The Child lacks Self- Confidence and Self Esteem.

The Child has difficulty functioning effectively, fears making mistakes, and anticipates receiving hurtful criticisms.
Negative Experiences
A Child is repeatedly ridiculed, humiliated, embarrassed, teased, insulted by Primary Caregivers, Peers, or Adults.
Supportive Measures Needed
Encouragement, compliments, recognition for his/her unique strengths and abilities.

Fear of Disapproval -- Sensitivity to Criticism
A Child feels rejected, inadequate, and discouraged.

A Child has low Self Esteem.
Negative Experiences
The Focus is on what the Child cannot do.

The Child is repeatedly subjected to hurtful criticisms, complaints, accusations, fault finding, unfavorable comparisons to others.

Supportive Measures Needed

CPR

Consistent, constructive, corrective positive reinforcement.

Compliments, praise, respect, reassurance, recognition for every small step on the road to achievement.

Focus on what the Child can do -- accentuate the Child's positive strengths, skills, and abilities.

Fear of Failure -- Fear of the Future, Fear of Change

The Child feels incompetent, unimportant, inferior to others.

The Child is unwilling to take risks, because he/she expects to fail.

The Child lacks will power, purpose, direction, self-confidence.

Negative Experiences

Primary Caregivers and/or teachers use pressure to impose unrealistic expectations upon a Child who is not ready to achieve such goals.

Supportive Measures Needed

Encouragement and support to achieve those goals that are realistically adjusted in accordance with his/her abilities.

Fear of Not Being Loved -- Jealousy

The Child feels threatened and resents the need to share Parental love and attention.

The Child fears that someone will take his/her place and regards Everyone as a rival.

The Child feels unloved, unappreciated, neglected, abandoned, and rejected.

Painful Experience

The arrival of a new sibling and the Fear of losing Parental love.

Supportive Measures Needed

The nurturing "a's"-- acceptance, acknowledgment, affection, appreciation, approval, attention.

Frequent physical and verbal reassurances -- plenty of daily hugs, kisses, smiles, praise.

Repression -- Fear of Self-Expression -- Blocked Communication

The Child has difficulty recognizing and expressing his/her true feelings.

The Child becomes tense and uptight.

The Child has problems coping with Worries and Fears.

The Child's ability to interact with other Children and Adults is impaired.

Negative Experience

The Child is taught that it is not okay to cry or freely express his/her Angry, hurt Feelings.

Supportive Measures Needed

Reassurances that it is okay to appropriately express Angry and hurt Feelings and is given opportunities to do so.

Consequences of Unresolved Childhood Fears

Fear stunts a Child's positive Physical and Emotional Growth.

Fear interferes with a Child's ability to concentrate.

Fear interferes with a Child's ability to develop or maintain healthy relationships.

Unresolved Childhood Fears affect a Child's ability to effectively function in the later years.

IMPORTANT TO NOTE:

A Child's Fears are not to be lightly dismissed or ignored.

A Child's Fears are not to be judged to be true or false, good or bad, right or wrong.

Children Need US TO Overcome Childhood Fears
Understanding, Unconditional Love
Security, a Sense of Success

SIGNS OF EMOTIONAL STRESS IN A CHILD'S HANDWRITING

Emotions Affect The Rhythm Of Finger Muscle Movements.

Finger action is controlled by two sets of Flexor Muscles -- the Extensors and the Retractors.

The Extensor Muscles extend the fingers to form upward strokes and rightward movements - rounded relaxed formations.

The Retractor Muscles contract the fingers to form downward strokes, leftward movements,- straight and angular formations.

When a Writer is in harmony with him/her Self, there is a smooth, continuous rhythmic flow of contractions and release movements across the page.

Anger, Fear, and Anxiety disrupt rhythmic muscle functioning.

Retractor Muscles remain taut and tense and prevent the Extensor Muscle Release Movement. This causes angular, narrow letter formations, closely spaced words, and crowded letters. This shows and tells that the Writer is tense, and has difficulty in expressing and coping with his/her Stressful Feelings.

Some variations in Slant, Sizing, Spacing and Letter Formations naturally occur and are expected. No page of writing contains Letter Formations that are uniform or identical in shape. However, too much variation lacks rhythmical balance and harmony.

RED ALERT SIGNALS!!!

Extremely heavy, strong Pressure, represented by very dark, thick pen strokes and deep impressions on the back of the paper, shows and tells that the Writer is tense, easily frustrated, aggressive, angry, and fearful.

If a Child's Handwriting suddenly becomes extremely small, microscopic, and illegible, the Child is troubled, unhappy, and is retreating into a world of his/her own. Illegibility shows and tells that the Writer is a poor communicator.

Tangling - overlapping of letters or lines of writing - and an extremely irregular, uneven, wobbly " up and down" Baseline shows and tells that the Child is anxious, moody, and frequently has "ups and downs"

Blotches, scratches, heavy cross-outs, strike-overs, jumbled, altered letters, and erasures, show and tell that a Child is feeling extremely anxious, confused, frustrated and fears making a mistake or doing something new.

Fear and Insecurity prevents a Child from freely expressing his/her thoughts and feelings. Any stroke within the circle letters – "a", "o", "d", "g",-interferes with open communication. The "secretive loop" within the right side of Circle Letters "a" and "o" shows that a Child keeps his/her private thoughts and feelings locked up and resists conversations with authority figures.

Closed "e" and "l" Listening Loops show an Auditory System Shut-down, a resistance to listen. Anger and Fear can cause an Auditory System Shut-down.

NOTE:

It Is Important To Keep An Ongoing Journal Of A Child's Handwriting Samples

-- to monitor the fluctuating dynamics of a Child's Emotional Growth and Development.

-- to identify the existence of any Red Alert Signals.

-- to determine if any Red Alert Signals are transitory or chronic in nature.

A combination of Red Alert Signals over an extended period of time shows and tells that a Child has a need to be heard and understood, and may require the attention and services of a Physical or Mental Health Professional.

WHY CHOOSING THE "WRITE WAY" TO RELEASE YOUR ANGRY SAD, ANXIOUS FEELINGS IS THE RIGHT WAY TO GO

It's the way to immediately relieve Emotional Stress and Physical Tension.

It's the safe way to make Peace with yourself and bring Closure to the Angry, Sad, Anxious Feelings that prevent You from Feeling Good about Yourself. The sooner You write out your Angry, Sad, Anxious Feelings, the better You will Feel because You are making room for Positive Thoughts to fill your Mind.

You can write out Angry, Sad, Anxious Feelings at any time of day or night.

You just need pen and paper and the Helping Hand below your wrist.

BE YOUR OWN BEST PEN PAL!!!

THE NEED FOR FORGIVENESS

FORGIVENESS is not about accepting, condoning, or agreeing with what caused you past pain.

FORGIVENESS is about ceasing to blame or feel resentment towards anyone for painful experiences suffered in the past.

FORGIVENESS is about letting go of sad memories.

FORGIVING is about giving yourself permission to get on with your Life.

FORGIVENESS is about coming to terms with what happened and taking Positive Action to heal, change, and move on.

FORGIVENESS is the key for Successful Survival - the first step for relieving Emotional Stress and restoring Physiological Balance to your Body Systems.

In Order To Grow, You Need To Let The Grudges Go.

The Trait Detector that shows and tells the presence of Resentment is a straight, inflexible initial stroke that begins at or below the Baseline.

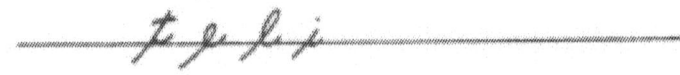

The Write Way To Release Resentment is to either eliminate the initial stroke or use a curved initial stroke at the Baseline.

Compile a Resentment List. Include the names of all Persons toward whom you feel resentment for past painful experiences.

Write a Letter to each Person on your Resentment List. Tell when and where the past painful experience took place. End your Letter with the following Forgive Statement:

I forgive You for all past painful experiences.

The Letter does not require mailing. The Letter serves as the Write Way to release the Feeling of Resentment that is living within You.

Examine the Initial Strokes of all Words in your Letter.

Rewrite each Word that shows a Resentment Stroke. Eliminate the Stroke as prescribed above. Practice writing the words each day for at least 30 consecutive days. It takes time to free yourself from the toxic Feeling of Resentment.

To avoid any Resentment build-up, constantly monitor the initial strokes of all letters.

If you detect the presence of Resentment, address the pain The Write Way, right away.

THE WRITE WAY TO RELEASE THE FEELING OF ANGER

Whenever You feel agitated, aggravated, annoyed, discontented, displeased, exasperated, frustrated, irritated or outraged, WRITE A LETTER TO A PERSON YOU WOULD LIKE TO SEE OR TALK TO.

State specifically - when, where, and what happened that caused you to feel Angry.

Use the word or words listed above that best describe your Angry Feelings.

I felt _____ when _____

_____
_____
_____
_____
_____
_____
_____
_____
_____
_____
_____
_____

After writing your LETTER, tear it up and throw it away. The LETTER has served its purpose. You have gotten rid of your Angry Feelings and made room for Good Feelings and Pleasant Thoughts.

Writing out your Angry Feelings before going to sleep allows your Body and Mind to relax, rest comfortably, and recharge itself with Positive Energy.

Regardless of the weather outside, you will rise and shine and be able to positively face the new day.

Note:

Before tearing up your LETTER, use the <u>Tally Sheet for</u> <u>GETTING IN TOUCH WITH YOUR ANGRY FEELINGS</u> <u>THROUGH YOUR "t-bars" and your "i-dots"</u> to see how well you score.

THE WRITE WAY TO HELP WORRY, DOUBT AND FEAR TO DISAPPEAR

Worry, Doubt, and Fear about future events causes one to ask "what if" questions.

Whenever You feel anxious, frightened, nervous, terrified, uptight, or worried about any future event, WRITE A WASTE LIST - A Worry, Anxiety, Stress and Tension List. List all the "what if's" you are afraid will happen.

_____

_____

_____

_____

_____

_____

_____

_____

_____

Write a reassuring response to your fearful "what if" questions.

Change the words "what if" to "even if" and complete the following statement.

Even if_____

were to happen, I can handle it, because I choose to believe that I have the inner strength and power to deal with whatever will come to be.

State at least 2 steps you can take to handle the situation, should that event happen.

I can_____

_____

_____

_____

I can_____

_____

_____

_____

Place your LIST in an envelope. Store your LIST in a safe place.

Refer to the envelope whenever the event happens.

BELIEVING THAT YOU CAN DEAL WITH WHATEVER HAPPENS IS THE KEY TO FEELING CONFIDENT, COMFORTABLE AND SECURE.

THE WRITE WAY TO RELIEVE SADNESS

Whenever You feel bored, confused, defeated, depressed, disappointed, discouraged, disgusted, downhearted, exhausted, lonely or unloved, write a letter to a person you would like to see or talk to.

Write about what makes You feel Sad. Use the word or words listed above that best describe your Feelings.

I feel_____
when I remember (state when, where, and what happened)

_____
_____
_____
_____
_____
_____
_____
_____
_____
_____
_____
_____
_____
_____
_____
_____
_____
_____
_____
_____

Your letter does not require mailing. The letter has served its purpose.

You have gotten rid of your Sad Feelings and made room for Good Feelings and Pleasant Thoughts.

THE IMPACT OF EMOTIONAL STRESS ON THE BODY SYSTEMS

Your Mind continuously and automatically communicates with your Body.

Your Body is designed to respond to all your Feelings within a fraction of a second.

When You experience stress to circumstances that anger, irritate, frighten, confuse, or endanger you, your Brain uses neurotransmitters as messengers to transmit this information to all Body Systems.

Your Nervous, Endocrine, Circulatory, and Immune Systems are alerted to respond to the stressful emergency.

Your Sympathetic Nervous System takes over.

Your Adrenal Glands release adrenaline into your bloodstream.

Your Pituitary Gland releases powerful hormones that make your blood pressure soar.

Sugar flows into your bloodstream for a quick burst of power.

There are chemical changes in the rate and intensity of the rhythmic functioning of your Heart, Lungs, and Digestive Tract.

Your Heart speeds up to pump the blood faster.

Your Lungs work faster and your breathing becomes rapid and shallow.

Your blood flow, containing needed oxygen, is switched away from your Skin and Digestive organs to your Brain and large leg muscles.

Your muscles contract and tighten up, causing increased muscle tension.

Your digestive process slows down to let your Body concentrate its energy on the stressful situation.

Your mouth feels dry - saliva is not being used for digestion.

Consequences of Intense, Prolonged Stress on the Body Systems

A weakened Immune System that lowers your Body's resistance to disease.

An exhausted Endocrine System that overloads your Body with stress hormones, creating hormonal imbalance and pain in vulnerable parts of your Body.

An overworked Sympathetic Nervous System, causing excessive muscle tension and pain in face, neck, chest, back, arms, legs.

A Digestive System shut-down that interferes with food absorption, causing depletion of vitamins, minerals, and proteins that are essential for the formation of Muscles, Hormones, Bones, Brain, and Nerve cells.

Interference with the elimination of toxic waste.

Sleep disturbances.

Excessive fatigue.

Inability to concentrate.

Illnesses that are linked to Intense, Prolonged Stress and Tension are allergies, backaches, diabetes, digestive disorders, heart disease, hypertension, respiratory ailments, skin disorders, tension headaches.

Physical pain is a response to a chemical imbalance, a deficiency, a weakness, an externally caused trauma, an emotional trauma, or a sustained injury, It is your Body's way of bringing a problem to your attention. Learn to listen to what your Body is telling you.

Ignoring the signals can intensify the pain.

LISTEN TO YOUR BODY SIGNALS

Your Body is a wonderful complex structure with an amazing power to heal itself.

Your Body needs your cooperation in order to function effectively and efficiently.

Your Body is constantly sending you signals.

Your Body lets you know when it needs nutritional energy. Signal is feeling of hunger.

Your Body lets you know when it is time for cell repair and revitalization. Signal is fatigue and drowsiness.

Your Body lets you know when something is wrong - an imbalance, a deficiency or weakness exists. Signal is pain and discomfort.

Failure to listen to your Body signals interferes with the state of your Health. Your Body becomes "run down". Pain increases in severity. The condition can become chronic.

Take Good Care Of The One Body That You Have For A Lifetime !!!

WINNING WAYS TO FEEL GOOD

THE POWER OF JOURNALING

THE POWER OF LAUGHTER

A MILE OF SMILES

MODERATE EXERCISE

THE COMFORT OF A HUG

PICTURE VISUALIZATION

VOWEL SOUND COUNT-OUT

THE POWER OF JOURNALING -- THE WRITE WAY TO ENRICH YOUR LIFE

Start a journal of "Happy Moments"
Make daily entries.
Date each entry.

Write about one or more events that made you feel that you had a Great Day.
Indicate specifically - when, where, and what happened.

Writing in your journal before going to sleep is a relaxing activity and is the right way to go for pleasant dreams.

Read your journal whenever you want to refresh your Memory and relive happy, exciting events. It's guaranteed to keep you smiling.

Share your Journal of "Happy Moments" with others.

THE POWER OF LAUGHTER

Laughter is the most inexpensive and most effective wonder drug.

Laughter is a universal medicine.

--Bertrand Russell

Laughter

Gives your Heart and Diaphragm Muscles a beneficial workout.

Improves your Circulation.

Fills your Lungs with oxygen-rich air.

Clears your Respiratory Passages.

Stimulates the release of Endorphins into your Bloodstream.

Reduces the tension in your Central Nervous System.

Learn to laugh at your mistakes.

Share amusing stories, anecdotes, and jokes that you have read, heard, or observed.

Laughter is the shortest distance between 2 People.

—Victor Borge

Laughter is free, legal, has no calories, no cholesterol no preservatives, no artificial ingredients and is absolutely safe.

--Dale Irvin

A MILE OF SMILES -- HIGHLY RECOMMENDED AS A DAILY EXERCISE

Relaxes your Facial Muscles.
Softens your Frown Lines.
Acts as a Natural Face Lift.
Produces a Positively Energized Environment when shared with others.

To increase your Smile Mileage
Place Yellow Smiling Face Stickers everywhere to serve as a reminder to Smile.
Enclose Smiling Stickers in personal correspondence.
Smile every time you look into the mirror!!!

A Smile is a curve that sets everything straight.
                                        --Phyllis Diller

Do You Know
It takes fewer Muscles to Smile than it does to Frown.

MODERATE EXERCISE -- MODERATE IN FREQUENCY AND DURATION

Increases the Blood and Oxygen Supply to your Heart and Lungs.

Lowers the level of Carbon Dioxide in your Lungs.

Lowers your Blood Pressure.

Relieves your Muscle Tension.

Increases your Metabolic Efficiency.

Improves your Learning Capacity.

Improves your Mood and ability to handle stressful situations.

Select an activity that you feel you will enjoy.

a 10 – 30 minute brisk walk, swimming, dancing, bicycling, yoga, tai-chi

Seek a place that offers you fresh air, sunshine, peace, and tranquility.

Do You Know
When you sweat, you are getting rid of harmful chemicals.

THE COMFORT OF A HUG -- A SIMPLE PAIN-FREE WORKOUT

A HUG is an important source of Comfort.

Aches and Pains need the Comfort of a Hug.

When you give and get a Hug, you establish a reciprocal flow of positive energy. By extending your arms, you instantly release Muscle Tension.

Give and get at least one Hug each day.

If no one is available, Hug yourself.

PICTURE VISUALIZATION

Enjoy the Spring Season all year round.

Surround yourself with pictures, posters, or paintings of scenes that celebrate Spring -- the Season of Renewal, Harmony, Peace, Hope, and Joy.

Visualize yourself within the setting.

Observe the Colors. Listen to the Sounds. Smell the Scents,

For Pleasant Dreams, view the picture/ poster before going to sleep.

To have a great day, view the picture /poster upon waking.

DEEP BREATHING and the VOWEL SOUNDS
"a", "e", "i", "o", "u".

Rx - For Defusing Anger, Fear, Sadness, or Depression
For restoring Inner Bio-Chemical Balance

Procedure - A Series of 5 Deep Breaths
Step 1 - Silently inhale to the count of 4.
Step 2 - Hold breath for the count of 2.
Step 3 - Audibly exhale to the count of 4, using one Vowel Sound.
Repeat Steps 1 - 3, using a different Vowel Sound each time.
The Series of 5 Deep Breaths can be repeated as many times as it takes for your Body Systems to cool down.
Use loosely extended fingers for counting.
Left hand fingers for inhale count.
Right hand fingers for exhale count.

5 Count Version
Step 1 - Silently inhale to the count of 5.
Step 2 - Hold Breath for the count of 2.
Step 3 - Audibly exhale to the count of 5, using each Vowel Sound per count out.

A RIDDLE TO THINK ABOUT

What is at the root of all your Beliefs and Attitudes?

What reflects your Experiences and your Feelings?

What determines how well you function and survive?

What is active from the first moment to the last moment of your Life?

What can change from moment to moment?

What never sleeps or rests?

What has the Power to Heal or Hurt?

What is unique for every Individual?

What can make you feel Comfortable and Self-Fulfilled and bring Love, Joy, and Peace into your Life?

What can provide the Strength, Courage, Confidence and Willpower you need to successfully achieve your Goals?

What can safely see you through difficult times?

What can make your day a good one -- every day?

Answer to the Riddle: Your Unique Inner Thoughts!!!

YOUR BRAIN --- A POWERFUL PERSONAL COMPUTER

Everyone is born with a Personal Computer that never sleeps --a Brain.

For your entire Lifetime, your Brain is the Processing Center for all your Knowledge and Experiences.

All information concerning what you hear, see, smell, taste, and touch is stored in your Brain's Memory Data Bank.

The information in your Memory Data Bank is stored and filed into either a Positive Energy Program or a Negative Energy Program.

The Positive Energy Program stores the Positive Thoughts and the Good Feelings of Joy, Love, and Hope.

The Negative Energy Program stores the Angry, Anxious, Sad Feelings and Thoughts.

You are the Programmer. Each day you have a choice -- to use the Positive Energy Program or the Negative Energy Program.

The Program you choose to use will determine the kind of day you will have.

To Have A Good Day, choose to Accentuate The Positive and Eliminate The Negative!!!

CHOICES

Do You Know?

Your Choices influence all your Life Experiences and determine how well you will function.

You are responsible for all the Choices you make in your lifetime.

Your Choices trigger, change, and set in motion Positive or Negative Thoughts.

Your Good Choices trigger your Positive Thoughts.

Your Positive Thoughts form your Positive Belief System.

Your Positive Belief System influences your Attitudes and your Behavior.

Choose to make Good Choices.

Choice Statements to Trigger Positive Thoughts and Beliefs

Choose Statements that are meaningful for you.

Write, Read, Say your selected Choice Statements every day for a minimum of 30 consecutive days.

Use the Simplified Printed "I" for all your written statements--A simple, single, straight, vertical downstroke.

-- I choose what is appropriate for me.
-- I choose to be responsible for my Choices.
-- I choose to make Good Choices about any part
-- of my life.
-- I choose what is best for maximum Body performance.
-- I choose to adapt my thoughts to the changes in my Body.
-- I choose to be Healthy.
-- I choose to do what it takes to be physically and emotionally fit.
-- I choose to be aware of any substances, stimuli, toxins that impair my Immune System.
-- I choose relaxation techniques appropriate for me to effectively reduce my Stress and Tensions.
-- I choose to control whatever I put into my mouth.

THE WRITE WAY TO A POSITIVE SELF-IMAGE AND BELIEF SYSTEM

When You have a Positive Self-Image and Belief System, You have the power and energy to form healthy relationships and function effectively in challenging situations.

Do You Know
The Personal Pronoun "I" is the only one letter word that represents the One most important Individual in the world.

The Personal Pronoun "I" is the only Pronoun that is always Capitalized. Capital letters are always used to signify importance.

A Positive Self-Image, A Sense of Self-Worth
The Key to Successful Social Relationships

The Key to a Positive Self-Image begins with having a Satisfying Relationship with One's Own Self.

You need to be
Self Accepting
Self Appreciating
Self Approving
Self Loving
Self Nurturing
Self Respecting
Self Trusting
Self Understanding

You need to accept and appreciate Yourself for who You are before You can accept others and have others accept You in return.

You need to feel love for Yourself before You can give love to others and get love in return.

You need to care for Yourself before You can care for others.

You need to feel respect for Yourself before You can respect others and get respect in return.

You need to understand Yourself before You can begin to understand others.

You need to value Yourself before You can value others.

A Positive Self-Image Empowers You To
Be A Positive Role Model.
Set A Good Example.
Relate Well With Others.

TAKE THE TIME TO BUILD A STRONG POSITIVE IMAGE!!!
A GOOD SELF-IMAGE LEADS TO GOOD SOCIAL RELATIONSHIPS!!!

The Write Way To Be the "I" You Want To Be

You are what you feel.   I feel that I am a winner!

You believe what you feel.   I believe that I am a winner!

You are what you believe.   I am a winner !

From the Glossary of Positive Adjectives choose 5 positive adjectives that describe the "I" you want to be.

For each word selected, complete the following 3 statements.
I feel that I am _____
I believe that I am _____
I am _____

Write and say each set of 3 statements, 3 times each, every day for at least 30 consecutive days.

It takes at least 30 consecutive days to successfully program your Positive Statements into your Memory Data Bank.

After 30 consecutive days, select another 5 adjectives and repeat the Programming Process. There is no limit to the number of adjectives that you may wish to include in your Belief System.

Say the Statements to yourself any time you want to Feel Good about Yourself.

YOU ARE WHO YOU BELIEVE YOU ARE!!!

Reminder:
It makes a difference where and how you cross your "t-bars".
Place the long, strong, evenly balanced t-bar close to the top of the "t-stem".

Glossary of Positive Adjectives

A --- agreeable, alert, ambitious, amiable
B --- brainy, brave, bright, brilliant
C --- capable, caring, charitable, charming, cheerful, competent, conscientious, cooperative
D --- dedicated, delightful, dynamic
E --- enthusiastic
F --- faithful, friendly
G --- generous, gentle, great
H --- helpful, healthy, honorable
I --- inquisitive, intelligent, interesting
J --- jolly, jovial, joyful, jubilant
K --- knowledgeable
L --- lively, lovable, loyal
M --- marvelous, mighty, mild-mannered, moral
N --- neat, neighborly
O --- outstanding
P --- patient, pleasant, polite
R --- reasonable, receptive, respectful, responsible
S --- satisfied, successful
T --- talented, thoughtful, tolerant, trustworthy, truthful
U --- understanding, unique, unselfish
V --- vibrant, victorious, vigorous, vivacious
W --- willing, witty, wonderful

Complete the following "I" statements by selecting a trait listed below. Use the color pen suggested for the trait selected.

I feel that I am _____.

I believe that I am _____.

I am _____.

Use orange ink for
courageous
sociable
constructive
confident
willing

Use yellow ink for
reasonable
logical
optimistic
articulate
forgiving
happy
organized

Use green ink for
balanced
efficient
methodical
appreciative
secure
contented
relaxed
at peace

Use purple ink for
proud
open-minded
worthy
accepting

Use blue ink for
reliable
accepting
flexible
tranquil
trusting

Use turquoise ink for
calm
changing
triumphant
certain

Use pink ink for
kind
supportive
considerate
compassionate
loving
sincere

Use red ink for
strong
determined
energetic

To reinforce your Positive Self Image

Say your "I" Statements in front of a mirror.

Smile.

Nod your head up and down. Avoid any side to side motion.

Add "yes" before each statement.

End each statement in an animated way -- with a "thumbs up" signal.

The Write Way to a Positive Belief System

Start your own Personal Daily Journal.

Date each entry.

Make an entry every day.

Choose from "I" STATEMENTS FOR POSITIVE ENERGY, those Thoughts that you want in your Memory Data Bank.

Select five Thoughts at a time.

WRITE - SEE - SAY the 5 Thoughts, 3 times each, for 30 days.

Use the simplified Printed "I" - a simple, single, straight, vertical downstroke - for all your written "I" Statements

Every 30 days, choose another 5 Thoughts to add to your entry.

Continue to increase the number of Thoughts so that the writing exercise lasts for 20/30 minutes.

Writing is a relaxing form of exercise.

Effective Programming Time for Journal Entries is shortly before going to sleep.

POSITIVE THOUGHTS PROVIDE POSITIVE ENERGY POWER!!!

"I" Statements for Positive Energy

I am the only one who is responsible for my thoughts and behavior.

I am responsible for my reactions to circumstances.

I am honest and open with myself.

I am discovering what it takes for me to feel good.

I am proud of myself.

I am at peace with myself.

I am comfortable with myself.

I am a kind and caring person.

I am consistent.

I am decisive.

I am a good listener.

I am in control of what passes my lips-- food going in and words coming out.

I accept myself for who I am.

I aim to be the best that I can be.

I appreciate all the good things that I can do.

I appreciate my uniqueness.

I believe in myself.

I believe that I have the courage and inner strength to get through difficult times.

I believe that I am an important Individual.

I believe that I count.

I believe that I am a Winner.

I believe that I am a good and deserving person.

I believe that I am a Success.

I believe that I can do anything that I make up my mind to do.

I believe that I have the power to solve my problems.

I have faith in my ability to achieve.

I hold no grudges.

I learn and grow from my mistakes.

I like who I am.

I respect myself.

I trust myself.

I value myself.

Teaching Values to Children starts with your own Ethical and Moral Codes of Beliefs and Behavior.

You need to feel it, believe it, and do it in order to teach it.

Write, Read, and Say the Value Statements.

Adding the word "yes" before each Statement gives the Statement an additional positive boost.

Value Statements

I am a caring person.

I am considerate of the feelings of others.

I am consistent in my positive feelings, beliefs, words, and actions.

I am forgiving of myself and others.

I am honest and open-minded.

I am reliable.

I am proud of myself.

I am willing to try the unfamiliar.

I assume responsibility for my own thoughts, actions, reactions to people and circumstances, and the consequences of my choices.

I have the courage to overcome fear and uncertainty.

I respect myself.

I respect the rights and beliefs of others.

I set appropriate and realistic limits and boundaries.

I take pride in myself, my accomplishments and my abilities.

I value myself and appreciate myself for who I am.

I value Human Life.

The ABC'S For Positive Thoughts and Action

Assume responsibility for strengthening your Positive Belief System.

Believe that you can successfully handle anything that comes your way, and you have the key to feeling Comfortable and Secure.

Clarify what is confusing by dealing with one issue at a time.

Detoxify what is toxic.

Focus on what you can do and not on what you can't do.

Fortify what is vulnerable.

Glorify Life, Love, and Laughter.

Identify which Feelings are at the root of your problems.

Justify what is valid.

Like what you have, rather than lament over what you do not have.

Modify what is extreme.

Nullify what is negative.

Pacify what is turbulent.

Rectify what is unbalanced.

Satisfy your unique Individual Needs -- safely and appropriately.

Simplify Life by breaking down what is complex into simple manageable steps.

Spend your time and energy seeking Joy and Satisfaction and there will be no room for Anger and Dissatisfaction.

Verify what are assumptions, inaccuracies, or speculations.

Zero in on your unique and special talents and abilities.

Positive Thinking creates change. Positive Action makes things happen.

Bottom line - P T A gives you P E P.

Positive Thoughts and Actions give you Positive Energy Power!!!

POSITIVE ENERGY IN ACTION

A PERSON WHO HAS POSITIVE ENERGY POWER
accepts responsibility for his/her own actions.
is broadminded.
chooses to be caring, consistent, cooperative.
communicates openly and honestly.
clearly defines feelings, goals, needs, values.
has strong determination to complete tasks and projects.
examines and evaluates facts and explores alternatives.
enjoys life.
is flexible, focused, and forgiving.
grows with each new experience.
has a healthy sense of humor.
has integrity and a positive Self-Image.
is kind and knowledgeable.
listens, learns, and loves to laugh.
is motivated to achieve and maintain inner peace of mind.
is non-judgmental.
is open-minded and optimistic.
has patience and self-pride.
questions wisely and specifically - what, when, where, how.
respects the rights of others and relates well socially.
smiles.
sets and achieves realistic goals.
is self-fulfilled.
seeks facts in order to find solutions.
trusts and triumphs.
takes positive action to make desired changes.
understands the meaning of Unconditional Love.
values him/her Self.
has vim, vigor, and vitality.
is a winner.
exercises in moderation.
is young in heart regardless of chronological age.

EMOTIONAL ENERGY is contagious!!! To "FEEL GOOD", seek to be with People who have Positive Energy Power. You can always tell a Person with Positive Energy Power by the smile that he/she is wearing.

THE POWER OF WORDS

The Words you choose to use form the Thoughts that express your Inner Feelings. Your Thoughts become your Belief System. What you believe affects your Attitude. Your Attitude affects your Behavior.

Food For Thought

Words generate Positive or Negative Emotional Energy. It takes one word a fraction of a second to bio-chemically change every cell in your Body and affect your Physical and Emotional State of Well-Being.

Words can divide or unite, hurt or heal. It never hurts to say a kind word because a kind word never hurts. Kind words win Peace. Angry words wage War.

WORDS HAVE THE POWER TO HURT

Sticks and stones can break one's bones
But words can hurt much more than stones.

Cruel, uncomplimentary words damage an Individual's Self-Esteem.

Individuals who experience uncontrollable Anger or Fear, use the tongue as a weapon to verbally attack and provoke Anger and Fear in others.

In the past, this kind of attack was referred to as a " tongue lashing". Today, this kind of attack is referred to as Verbal Abuse.

The words used for verbal attack tend to be inaccurate and uncomplimentary. They tend to be names and descriptive labels that criticize, demean, discredit, ridicule, insult, and humiliate an Individual's abilities, appearance, or physical build. Some commonly used labels are: stupid, dumb, moron, idiot, fool, crazy, lazy, worthless, clumsy, careless, miserable, selfish, failure, ugly, fat, slob, animal.

Hurtful words severely threaten a Child's Security and Self-Esteem.

The effects of repeated criticisms:

A Child becomes hypersensitive to even constructive criticism.

A Child becomes critical of His/Her Self and can retaliate by becoming negatively critical of others.

A Child withdraws or retreats from others.

Teasing about issues over which a Child has no control, destroys his/her Self-Confidence.

Ridicule makes a Child feel inadequate, unworthy, and uncomfortable.

Unfavorable Comparisons create feelings of Inferiority, and Self-Doubt, and generate a negative competitive attitude based on Anger, namely, "beat all others to get to the top to be powerful".

Children who repeatedly hear Negative Messages, begin to believe that the words are true and will act them out. What you believe, will be!!!

Words that have stood the test of time. "If you can't say anything positive, then it is time to say nothing at all."

Repeated use of cruel words is a destructive, no-win means of communication.

The Person sending the Negative Message does not feel good. The Person receiving the Negative Message does not feel good.

Become a Positive Message Sender

Increase the number of Positive Messages you send.

Make a list of the hurtful words you frequently use.

Supply the antonym for each word and you have an Instant Positive Word Vocabulary available for you to use.

Examples:

hate	love
dislike	like
fail	succeed
disrespect	respect

Become a Selective Listener when you are the Receiver of Negative Messages.

Silently repeat the following Messages to yourself as often as necessary.

The Messages will serve as a successful defense strategy to tune out the effects of the verbal attack.

I can not control the thoughts or actions of others.

I can control how I respond to others.

I do not take the attack personally.

It is not about me.

I am not the cause of the problem.

I have nothing to do with it.

I know the inaccurate, untrue words are the expressions of an angry, insecure Individual whose Feelings are out of control.

Instant Rephrasing Replacing Negative Words With Positive Words

Rx - For those Individuals suffering from Positive Word Deprivation caused by chronic, intense, toxic Negative Word Overload.

Treatment Procedure
Consult your Dictionary to perform an immediate Word Transfusion to increase Positive Word Power.

Enter all newly acquired Positive Words into a Personal Positive Word Power Journal.

Replace any existing Negative Vocabulary Words that you frequently use with their Antonyms.

There is a Positive Word for every Negative Word.

Seek Synonyms for Positive Words in order to strengthen your Positive Word Power.

Prognosis
Immediate increase in level of Positive Energy.

Fortified Positive Energy allows you to successfully deal with any daily occurrences of Negative Pain and prevent toxic Negative Overload.

Procedure is completely safe and non-toxic.

There is no danger of overdosing.

Challenge:
How quickly can you recognize a negative word and thought?

How quickly can you rephrase to a positive word and thought?

Your speed and detector skills increase with practice.

Become a Super Word Detector!!!

Use The Prefix Way to Increase Your Positive Word Vocabulary

For words that are positively not "in", drop the negative prefix "in" and the words are in to win.

inattentive	attentive
inconsistent	consistent
inappropriate	appropriate
incapable	capable
incompetent	competent
insecure	secure
insincere	sincere
intolerant	tolerant

Words that are "in" and that give you Positive Energy Power

initiative   interest   introspection

Words that you can positively undo by dropping the negative prefix "un"

unaccountable	accountable
unaware	aware
uncaring	caring
uncertain	certain
uncomfortable	comfortable
uncommunicative	communicative
undisciplined	disciplined
unfriendly	friendly
unhealthy	healthy
uninformed	informed
unrealistic	realistic
unsatisfactory	satisfactory
unwilling	willing

The Write Way to Provide Positive Closure to Negative Statements

Use the antonym connection word "but".

"but" joins 2 thoughts together.

The second thought contradicts the first thought.

When writing statements that express Worry, Uncertainty, Anxiety, Pessimism, Fear, Discouragement, Hopelessness, use any of the following Positively Energized Thoughts to complete your statement.

but I'll do my best.

but I can handle it.

but I can do it.

but it will be okay.

but I can get through it.

but I will work it out.

Examples:

I feel Discouraged, but I will work it out.

I feet Sad, but I can get through it.

BASICS FOR EFFECTIVE COMMUNICATION AND SATISFYING RELATIONSHIPS

Your Feelings, Words, and Actions must match. Say what you really feel and mean. Mean what you say. Do what you say you mean.

Focus on Accuracy. Seek answers to "who", "what", "when", "where", "how".

Focus on One specific at a time - a specific behavior, condition, event, feeling, issue, need, problem, situation, or Individual.

Beware of words that fail to be specific or accurate - generalizations, speculations, rumors, gossip, hearsay.

An Individual can only speak from his /her own viewpoint, which is based upon his/her own unique experiences, ideas, beliefs, feelings.

Each Individual is entitled to express his/her own opinions.

"I" messages express your viewpoint and do not lead to confrontations.

Sentence starters for accurate stress-free communication:

In my opinion, _____

From my point of view, _____

I believe_____

I feel_____

I think_____

Beware of messages that begin with the word "You". "You" messages point an accusing finger and generate feelings of resistance and hostility.

Every Individual needs his/her Feelings acknowledged, accepted, heard, understood, and validated.

Be a PAL -- a Patient, Accurate Listener. By accepting the fact that each Individual is entitled to his/her own unique viewpoint, you are allowing the Speaker to verbally express his/her Angry, Sad, Anxious Feelings in a safe non-threatening environment. Maintain eye contact. Focus on the words that reflect the Speaker's inner feelings. Words are subject to individual interpretation To avoid misinterpretation, it is important for the listener to clarify and confirm his/her understanding as to the accuracy of the message heard.

Sentence starter for accurate clarification:

It seems to me that you are feeling_____

because _____.

The Speaker can agree or disagree. If the Speaker disagrees, further clarification is needed.

After the Speaker has finished expressing his/her feelings, offer support and encouragement. Ask, "What can I do to help?"

Important To Note:

The role of a PAL is not to advise, agree, analyze, approve, comment, correct, criticize, discredit, evaluate, interrupt, judge, or tease.

The Write Way To Negotiate A Commitment For Change

Set aside a time for a Meeting for All, who are involved.

Prior to the Meeting, list, specifically, what responsibilities you need your Child to assume -- changes that you need to have take place.

At the Meeting, discuss the List of Needs with your Child, asking, which <u>ONE</u> Need he/she thinks is the most reasonable to focus in on.

Agree as to when, where, and how the change will take place.

Negotiate as to what rewards will be earned for following through on the Agreement.

Indicate what the Consequences will be for not following through on the Agreement. Consequences are to be appropriate, and within reasonable time limits.

At the Meeting, give your Child an opportunity to express what he/she needs from you and determine which-ONE Need can be satisfied.

Agree as to when, where, and how the change will take place.

Schedule a specific time for Weekly Meetings to see if the Agreement requires any revision. If so, modify the conditions.

Post copies of the Agreement wherever it is convenient.

A Written Agreement
-- provides structure.
-- prevents Emotional Confrontation because attention is being focused on the Agreement.
-- opens the lines for Parent/Child Communication. Each has the opportunity to express his/her Needs.

IMPORTANT NOTE: WORK ON ONE CHANGE AT A TIME!!! PATIENCE AND CONSISTENCY ARE ESSENTIAL!!!

THE RIGHT WAY TO
SOLVE YOUR PROBLEMS

Problems are here to stay. They are a part of Life.

Problems are as unique as Individuals.

What is a problem for one person, may not be a problem for another person.

You have a problem when you experience feelings of Anxiety, Fear, Frustration, Anger, Sadness, or Guilt.

You are the only One who really knows when You have a problem.

You are the only One who really knows how You feel.

You are the only One who can identify, define and solve your problem.

The shortest distance between identifying problems and reaching realistic solutions is keeping your eyes focused on specific facts, issues, circumstances, actions.

Specific questions that can help you to identify, define your problem issues and yield solutions are: "what" and "when"

What is my problem?

What realistic Positive Action am I willing to take to solve my problem?

When is the appropriate time to begin my Positive Action Plan?

When is the appropriate time to evaluate the success of my Positive Action Plan?

Every solution is always subject to change, revision, and improvement.

Life is in a constant state of flux. Nothing ever stays the same.

Problems are challenges -- opportunities for change, growth, and discovery.

EACH PROBLEM SOLVED IS A VICTORY!!!

IMPORTANT NOTE!!!

Do not make a POSITIVE ACTION PLAN when you are angry, fearful, or frustrated. Negative reactions cause a chemical imbalance in your Body Systems, and interfere with your ability to plan Positive Action.

Take time out to restore your chemical balance. Take slow deep breaths. Calm down. Relax. Then, plan your Positive Action.

THE WRITE WAY TO POSITIVELY ENERGIZED PERSONALITY (PEP) TRAITS

Your Personality Traits are reflected in your handwriting.

Learn the 8 Letter Shapes that show and tell that a Writer is a Super Communicator with High Self Esteem.

For Confidence, Will Power and High Self Esteem
"t- bars" that are long, strong, evenly balanced, and crossed close to the top of the "t" stem.

To Be A Super Communicator
"a's" and "o's" that are clean uncluttered circles.
"e's" and "l's" that have moderately-rounded listening loops.

For Accuracy, Improved Memory and Observational Skills
"i's" and "j's" whose dots are placed close to their stems.

To Feel Socially Comfortable
"m's" with humps that are descending or even in height.

LEARNING TO WRITE THE ESTEEM TEAM LETTER SHAPES CAN GIVE YOU POSITIVE ENERGY POWER
(PEP) !!!

IT DOES MATTER HOW AND WHERE YOU CROSS YOUR "t's"!!!

You are only a line away from having Self-Confidence and Strong Will Power.

"t-bars" that are long, strong, evenly balanced and placed close to the top of the "t-stem," show and tell that the Writer has Self-Confidence, High Self Esteem, sets achievable Goals, and has the WillPower to overcome everyday obstacles.

WILLPOWER TRANSLATES WISHES INTO ACTION!!!

THE WRITE WAY TO RAISE YOUR LEVEL OF CONFIDENCE AND WILLPOWER

Use 8 1/2 size paper.

Practice writing the Key Words and Sentences for 20 minutes a day for 30 consecutive days. It takes a minimum of 30 days to Program a new Habit into your Memory Data Bank.

After each Practice Session, check for accuracy of the "t-bar" placement.

Successful Programming into your Memory Data Bank requires a minimum of 30 consecutive accurate entries.

NOTE:

It takes Time to form new Habits.

The length of Time to learn a new Habit varies for each Person. For some, it may be a month. For some, it may be several months.

KEY WORDS FOR SUCCESSFUL PROGRAMMING: (C P R) CONSISTENCY -- PATIENCE -- REPETITION

THE WRITE WAY TO "t-bars"
THAT SHOW AND TELL
SELF -CONFIDENCE AND WILLPOWER

Long, strong, evenly balanced "t-bars" are placed close to the top of the "t-stem".

KEY WORDS
triumph
strength
trust
time

KEY STATEMENTS
I take the time to set realistic goals.
I take the time to appreciate my achievements.
I take the time to do my best.
I trust in my strength and ability to triumph.
I feel great about me.
I have strong faith and belief in myself.

MODERATELY ROUNDED "e" and "l" Loops and
WELL-ROUNDED, CLEAR "a's" and "o's"
CAN SHARPEN YOUR LEARNING, LISTENING, AND
COMMUNICATING SKILLS

THE WRITE WAY TO BE A PAL
(A PATIENT, ATTENTIVE LISTENER)

Use 8 1/2 size paper.

Practice writing the Key Words and Sentences for 20 minutes a day for 30 consecutive days. It takes a minimum of 30 days to Program a new Habit into your Memory Data Bank.

After each Practice Session, check the shape of the "e" and "l" loops, and the "a" and "o" circles.

Successful Programming into your Memory Data Bank requires a minimum of <u>30 consecutive accurate entries.</u>

NOTE:

It takes Time to form new Habits.

The length of Time to learn a new Habit varies for each Person.

For some, it may be a month. For some, it may be several months.

KEY WORDS FOR SUCCESSFUL PROGRAMMING:
CONSISTENCY -- PATIENCE – REPETITION (CPR)

THE WRITE WAY FOR CLEAR CIRCLE LETTERS AND LISTENING LOOPS TO FORM THE LINES FOR HONEST OPEN COMMUNICATION

a's . . o's . . e's . l's .

Well-rounded clear, uncluttered circle letters "a" and "o" show and tell that the Writer is broadminded, and honest.

Moderately rounded "e" and "l" loops show and tell that the Writer is an attentive listener, open-minded, and willing to accept new ideas.

Key Words
respect
learn
listen
look
observe
open, honest communication

Key Statements

I respect myself and others.

I can learn a great deal when I listen to new ideas.

I am learning to enjoy each day.

I listen with respect to the opinions of others, even though I may not agree with their views.

I am able to be a good listener.

I thoughtfully evaluate all aspects of an issue.

I communicate when I openly express my Inner Feelings.

I am an open, honest Communicator.

YOU ARE ONLY A DOT AWAY
FROM IMPROVING YOUR MEMORY

"i" and "j" dots placed close to their stems show and tell that the Writer has a good Memory, is observant, dependable, loyal, and faithful to one's ideals.

THE WRITE WAY TO IMPROVE YOUR MEMORY
Use 8 1/2 size paper.

Practice writing the Key Words and Sentences for 20 minutes a day for 30 consecutive days. It takes a minimum of 30 days to Program a new Habit into your Memory Data Bank.

After each Practice Session, check for accuracy of the "i" and "j" dot placement.

Successful Programming into your Memory Data Bank requires a minimum of <u>30 consecutive accurate entries,</u>

<u>NOTE</u>:
It takes Time to form new Habits.

The length of Time to learn a new Habit varies for each Person.

For some, it may be a month. For some, it may be several months.

KEY WORDS FOR SUCCESSFUL PROGRAMMING: (CPR) CONSISTENCY -- PATIENCE – REPETITION. (CPR)

THE WRITE WAY FOR – "i" - AND – "j" DOTS TO BE ATTENTIVELY LOYAL TO THEIR STEMS

"i" and "j" Dots are placed close to their stems.

Key Words

attention	just
details	joy
ideals	joint
interest	

Key Statements

It is in my best interest to pay attention to what I do.

I believe it is important to enjoy each day.

When I pay attention to details, I can remember what it is I see.

I join in activities just for the joy of it.

Every joint in my body feels my joy.

Each day, I am learning that the number of pleasures to enjoy in Life are just infinite.

EVEN OR DESCENDING "m" HUMPS CAN MAKE YOU FEEL SOCIALLY COMFORTABLE.

THE WRITE WAY TO FEEL POISED

Use 8 1/2 size paper.

Practice writing the Key Words and Sentences for 20 minutes a day for 30 consecutive days. It takes a minimum of 30 days to Program a new Habit into your Memory Data Bank.

After each Practice Session, check the shape of the "m" humps

Successful Programming into your Memory Data Bank requires a minimum of 30 consecutive accurate entries.

NOTE:

It takes Time to form new Habits.

The length of Time to learn a new Habit varies for each Person.

For some, it may be a month. For some, it may be several months.

KEY WORDS FOR SUCCESSFUL PROGRAMMING: (CPR) CONSISTENCY -- PATIENCE -- REPETITION

The Write Way for Many Moments of Emotional Ease

Even or descending height of "m" humps show and tell that the Writer has poise, is tactful and considerate of others.

Key Words
diplomacy
maximum
momentum

Key Statements
I make the most of my time.

I do not make mountains out of molehills.

I am able to overcome major obstacles when I make up my mind to do so.

I create miles of smiles for myself when I think of the many pleasant memories stored in my mind.

Confidence in myself gives me momentum to achieve.

I feel good about myself.

I maximize the positive and minimize the negative.

THE ABC'S FOR CREATING A SAFE, NURTURING HOME ENVIRONMENT

Accept each Child for what he/she is, not what you want him/her to be.

Allow each Child to grow at his/her own rate of readiness and development.

Allow each Child the opportunity to verbally express his/her Angry Feelings in order to avoid Toxic Emotional Build-Up.

Appreciate the uniqueness of each Child. Each Child has his/her own unique features, bio- chemical profile, personality traits, experiences, beliefs, viewpoint, fingerprints, and handwriting style. No Person is or can be exactly like anybody else.

Avoid making assumptions before the facts are known.

Be Aware:

A Child's Learning and Communication Skills begin on the first day of Life.

The 5 Senses -- Sight, Smell, Hearing, Taste, Touch -- are the sources for his/her Learning Experiences.

A Child's cry is the first sign of Communication to express a need for attention -- food, discomfort.

Babies are sensitive to Touch. Touch provides a basic connection with other people. A hug helps to relieve a Sense of Isolation, and offers Comfort and Support.

A Child's experiences within the first 7 years of Life, strongly influence his/her ability to socially interact with others in later life.

A Child understands Language before his/her ability to use it.

A Child learns how to handle Feelings of Anger, Frustration, and Fear by observing the behavior of Parents, Significant Other Adults, Peers, and the Multi-Media.

A Child learns Love by receiving it.

A Child needs to know by a Parent's Words and Actions that he/she is loved and respected. Courtesy and Consideration tell a Child that he/she is important.

A Child needs a safe, non-judgmental, non-threatening environment in order to learn.

A Child has a strong need for Belonging. There is no need for a Child to roam when Unconditional Love, Safety, Support, and Understanding exists in the home.

A Child confides in someone only if he/she feels it is safe to do so.

A Parent's Relationship with each Child is unique. It can never be duplicated or replaced.

The birth of a sibling is the birth of Sibling Rivalry -- competition for Parental Attention. To decrease the need for a Child to use quarreling as an attention-getting device, give each Child special time. Avoid making comparisons. Give attention to appropriate behavior.

Be consistent in Words and Actions. Mean what you say. Say what you mean. Do what you say you mean. It is important to practice what you teach. You cannot succeed in teaching Values -- Codes of Behavior -- if double standards prevail. "Do as I say, not as I do" sends a mixed message, breeds inconsistency and confusion. Be flexible in order to achieve and maintain Moderation, Harmony, and Balance.

Be willing to Forgive. Forgiveness releases Emotional Pain

Be willing to Share your Inner Feelings and Thoughts with your Child.

Be willing to Negotiate and Compromise in order to resolve conflicts.

Be a PAL -- a Patient, Attentive Listener.

Clarify and Simplify all messages. Indicate "what," "when," "where" "how." End all messages and statements on a positive note. The last few words one hears are often what is remembered.

Demonstrate daily affection with hugs and smiles galore!!! A hug is an important source of comfort. When you give and get a hug, you establish a reciprocal flow of Positive Energy.

Discipline in private. Discipline is a Corrective Action to teach more appropriate behavior. It is important for a Child to understand what a Parent considers and defines to be unacceptable behavior and what are the immediate consequences for such behavior. Consequences are to be relative and reasonable, and not associated with Anger or Revenge. Eliminate Emotional Warfare. Address one specific issue at a time.

Eliminate a Parent/Child Power Struggle. Set up a Written Schedule for time allotted for daily activities. A Written Schedule provides for Organization, Structure, Stability, and Consistency. Prepare your Child 2 - 5 minutes before the anticipated change of activity to allow the Child to comfortably make a transition.

"In -- minutes, it will be time to_____."

Referring to a clock or timer serves as an objective reminder for switching activities.

Encourage an "I can do it" attitude to strengthen a Child's Self-Confidence.

Encourage curiosity.

Encourage Reasonable Order and Organization to prevent accumulated clutter and eliminate endless hours of search, confusion, anger and anxiety.

Establish Reasonable Rules. Rules are to take into consideration the temperament and age of the Child. Rules are to be readjusted to accommodate for new circumstances. Rules are to be consistently enforced. Reasonable consequences for broken rules are to be clearly understood.

RULE #1 in every Household

NO ONE GOES TO BED FEELING ANGRY!!

Feelings are responses /reactions to experiences. Happiness, Hope, and Joy are responses to pleasant, satisfying experiences.

Anger, Fear, Sadness, and Depression, are reactions to traumatic experiences. You must feel good about yourself in order to transfer that feeling to a Child. Your feelings about your Child are not caused by what he/she does, but by what you think about what he/she does.

Feelings are not to be judged to be right or wrong, good or bad, true or untrue, real or imagined. It is important not to minimize what a Child feels!

Focus on what can be done, instead of on what can't be done.

Follow- through on all Commitments and Promises. By keeping your word, a Child learns to trust.

Honor a Child's Independence

Lessen the opportunity for conflict and confrontation by lessening the tendency to say "no" before thinking things through.

Lighten up with Laughter.

Notice and Value Positive Behavior. A Child will repeat behavior that gets attention.

Offer Constructive Correction to achieve Positive Change.

Prevent Frustration and Rebellion by providing appropriate answers at the time questions are raised.

Provide Pleasurable Learning Experiences to encourage Positive Emotional Growth.

Quell your Child's qualms by taking time to listen to his/her Needs and Feelings.

Respect a Child's Privacy. Each Child requires his/her own Space. A Child's Personality determines the amount of Space required for Comfort.

Respond to a Child's wrongdoing by focusing on how to do better in the future, rather than labeling what is past.

Set Appropriate Boundaries and Limits to avoid Extremes, Misunderstandings, and Confusion.

Talk quietly and calmly and a Child will tune in to your message. Yelling turns off a Child's Listening Power.

Trying to talk a Child out of a Temper Tantrum, intensifies the emotion and shows the Child that poor behavior gets attention. Instead, remove yourself from the room. Few children maintain Tantrums without an audience.

Teach your Child:

There are at least two alternatives, options, choices to every situation.

Each One is responsible for his/her own Feelings, Words, Thoughts, Beliefs, Attitudes, Actions, Successes, and Failures.

Each One is responsible for the way he/she chooses to react to People, Situations, and Events.

Each Human Being is entitled to his/her own Point of View.

Each Human Being has Strengths and Weaknesses.

Each Human Being has Value.

Each Human Being is different but equal.

Each Human Being can make a difference.

Unconditional Love accepts and values a Child regardless of what he/she accomplishes or achieves.

Use C P R to build a Child's Self-Esteem. Compliment -- Praise -- Recognize – Reward what is achieved, what is attempted, what is correct, what is unique.

Zero in on the Positive Side of Mistakes. All Human Beings make mistakes. A mistake is a signal that a deficiency or weakness exists. A mistake is an opportunity to identify where the deficiency exists, and to learn what Positive Action will prevent a recurrence. Mistakes serve as stepping stones to Learning, Growing, Achieving.

Beware of the Hazards to a Child's Emotional Health

Any traumatic, painful situation, event, experience -- deprivation, neglect, abuse, abandonment -- generates Emotional Insecurity -- Anxiety, Anger, Fear, Distrust.

A Child who is denied Unconditional Parental Love develops an insatiable need for Love, can become promiscuous to prove that he/she is worthy of Love, can resist Authority and misbehave, can seek attention from negatively energized sources, feels lonely, angry, and pretends not to care.

A Child who feels abandoned, abused, or neglected, feels betrayed and is not able to trust others.

A Parent's unwillingness to take the time to communicate and address a Child's needs, makes a Child feel unwanted.

A Parent, who demands perfection from a Child, sets an impossible standard, and sets Self and Child up for Failure.

A Child who tries to measure up to parental dreams and impossible expectations can suffer from severe Anxiety and Depression.

Extremes in Parental Discipline adversely affect a Child's Self-Esteem.

Permissiveness - a lack of discipline - reflects a lack of caring and love.

An Authoritarian Attitude does not accept a Child's Individuality, ignores the right of a Child to explore his/her own Feelings, breeds Resentment and Rebellion, tells a Child what to do and how to feel by making demands, and imposing "should's," "ought's," "must's," "don't" "stop's."

Overly Strict Discipline imposes punishment that continues to hurt a Child's Self Worth. A Child who is afraid of severe punishment from his/her Parents will deny, lie, or hide from mistakes.

Ignoring a Child's developmental needs, places a Child at risk, leads to Emotional Stress and Learning Problems.

Inconsistency in Words and Actions, breeds Fear and Insecurity.

Most power struggles between a Parent and Child are over issues that Parents cannot really control but want to control.

A Parent who imposes his/her own interests and preferences, stifles a Child's Initiative and Creativity, and damages a Child's Confidence.

A Parent who uses ridicule, nagging, scolding, or sarcasm, acts out of Anger, Hostility, and feelings of Helplessness.

Over scheduling of After-School Activities leads to Emotional Stress.

Overemphasis on Grades leads to Emotional Stress.

Overprotection stifles a Child's Emotional Growth.

Ridiculing a Child's facial and body features, destroys a Child's Self-Confidence.

Teasing severely damages a Child's Self- Esteem and breeds Anger, Frustration, Resentment.

Use of Violence to correct Violent behavior fosters continued Violence.

When a Parent says hurtful things to a Child, the Parent hurts the Child, and teaches the Child how to be hurtful.

TIMELY FACTS

Every Living Thing in the Universe is governed by Time.

All activities, events, and experiences are measured in terms of seconds, minutes, hours and days.

Everyone has the same number of minutes and hours in a day -no more - no less.

Time constantly moves forward (except when time reverts from Daylight Savings Time, or when travelling to another Time Zone). With each passing moment, Tomorrow becomes Today.

Each Individual has his/her own unique inner Biological Clock, Sense of Timing, and Body Rhythm.

Your Sense of Timing depends on your unique basic Personality Temperament.

Your glands produce hormones and chemicals that control your unique inner 24-hour Biological Clock, and determine how many hours your Body needs for sleeping, waking, eating. Sufficient rest is essential to balance your inner Body Rhythm. Your timing is off when you begin too soon, too late, or spend too much time in one area of activity. To relieve Stress, schedule reasonable and realistic periods of time to eat, work, sleep, relax, and exercise.

If You spend too much Time thinking about past painful issues, You are governed by feelings of Anger. If You spend too much Time thinking about events that will happen in the future, You are governed by Fear.

The best Time to express hurt feelings, is the moment it occurs -- before the pain has time to turn to chronic Anger, Fear or Depression.

Time spent seeking Joy and Satisfaction leaves no room for Anger and Dissatisfaction.

When You make Peace with the Painful Past, You can then move on to a Peaceful Present.

The only Time that changes can be made is in the Powerful Present. Once a moment passes, it is History. One cannot change History.

Do not waste Time today on issues that You cannot control. You can only control what is inside your own Body and your own Mind - your own Feelings, Thoughts, and Behavior - your own Words and your own Actions.

Respect the importance of Time.

Each moment is an opportunity that is never repeated.

It takes one moment to initiate a change that can affect the direction of your whole Life.

It takes one shared moment to change relationships.

It takes one moment to provide the Hope for a good Tomorrow.

Successful outcomes are based upon good choices and good timing. Good timing requires realistic planning.

Time, Patience, and Practice makes everything better.

Time seems to fly when you are with Positively Energized People in a Positively Energized Environment.

When You make the best use of your time, You are sure to have the Time of your Life.

As long as You have Life, there is Time to:

Appreciate who You are and what You have.

Believe in yourself.

Discover your needs and defuse your level of Stress and Tension.

Experience the joys of life.

Free yourself from the painful feelings of Anger, Sadness, Fear.

Initiate Positive Action.

MNEUMONICALLY SPEAKING – MEANINGFUL CONCEPTS WITHIN THE LETTERS OF A WORD

What Is Within A Satisfying Relationship

R   Respect, Responsibility
E   Enthusiasm
L   Love
A   Acceptance of what is
T   Trust
I   Insight
O   Open-mindedness
N   Nurturing, nature
S   Safety, Stability, Smiles
H   Healthy Sense of Humor
I   Integrity
P   Patience, Positive Attitude

The Positives To Be Found In Success

S   Self- Awareness
U   Understanding
C   Compassion, Constructive Choices
C   Courage, Competence
E   Esteem for One's Self
S   Self- Confidence
S   Serenity

What Is To Be Found In A Good Life

L   Learning, Listening, Loving, Laughing
I   Ideas, Independence, Integrity, Insight
F   Freedom From Fear And Frustration
E   Enjoyable Experiences

The Positives To Be Found When You Cope
C   Courage, Confidence, Constructive Change
O   Open- Mindedness
P   Positive Energy
E   Enlightenment

Issues Important To Focus In On
F   Feelings, Facts
O   Options, Order, Organization
C   Consistent Constructive Change
U   Understanding
S   Specifics

Everyone Needs Emotional Support Plus Care.
S   Stability
U   Unconditional Acceptance
P   Praise
P   Pleasure
O   Optimistic Outlook
R   Respect, Recognition
T   Trust

P   Patience
L   Love
U   Unconditional Understanding
S   Security

C   Compassion
A   Attention, Appreciation
R   Reassurance
E   Encouragement

It Is Better To Act Rather Than React
A   Acknowledge, Achieve
C   Cope, Change To Constructive Choices
T   Think Logically, Triumph

R   Resist Change
E   Exercise Excuses, Exaggerate
A   Avoid Relevant Issues
C   Complain, Condemn, Criticize
T   Tend To Tease Or Threaten

To Be Found In Positively Energized Self- Esteem
S   Serenity, Security
E   Empowerment
L   Love, Laughter
F   Fulfillment

E   Enjoyment
S   Success
T   Trust, Triumphs
E   Enlightenment
E   Enthusiasm
M   Momentum

For SOS, Use CPR
S   Security
O   Order
S   Stability, Structure

C   Commitment, Consistency, Constructive Choices
P   Patience, Practice, Persistence
R   Repetition, Reinforcement

TWENTY TIPS ON HOW TO FEEL GOOD ABOUT YOURSELF

A MANUAL FOR PRE-TEENS AND ADOLESCENTS

Feelings - Your Source For Emotional Energy

Human Beings function and survive on Emotional Energy --
FEELINGS

Feelings influence what You Think.

What You Think influences what You Believe.

What You Believe Influences how You Act.

How You Act influences Your Relationships with Others.

Positive and Negative Feelings cannot occupy the same space
in the same Body at the same time.

Only one Feeling can be expressed at any one time.

When You feel Love, You do not feel Anger.

When You feel Happy, You do not feel Sad.

When You feel Secure, You do not feel Fear.

When You smile, You do not frown.

When You hug, You do not fight.

When You laugh, You do not cry.

When You feel Comfortable, You like the way You feel.
You feel good about Yourself. You like who You are. You
believe that You are a Winner.

You are proud of Yourself. You appreciate all the good
things that You can do. You take good care of Yourself. You
aim to be the best that You can be. You feel Happy!!!

When You feel Uncomfortable, You don't like the way You
feel. You don't feel good about Yourself. You don't like who
You are. You don't believe that You are a Winner. You are not
proud of Yourself. You don't appreciate all the good things that
You can do. You don't take good care of Yourself. You don't
aim to be the best that You can be. You do not feel Happy!!!

HAPPY FEELINGS SUPPLY YOUR MIND AND BODY WITH
THE POSITIVE ENERGY THAT YOU NEED TO FEEL GOOD
ABOUT YOURSELF!!!

WHY CHOOSING "THE WRITE WAY" TO RELEASE YOUR ANGRY, SAD, ANXIOUS, FEELINGS IS THE RIGHT WAY TO GO.

It's the way to immediately relieve Emotional Stress and Physical Tension.

It's the safe way to make Peace with yourself and bring Closure to the Angry, Sad, Anxious Feelings that prevent You from Feeling Good about Yourself. The sooner You write out your Angry, Sad, Anxious Feelings, the better You will Feel because You are making room for Positive Thoughts to fill your Mind.

You can write out Angry, Sad, Anxious Feelings at any time of day or night.
You just need pen and paper and the Helping Hand below your wrist.

BE YOUR OWN BEST PEN PAL!!!

THE WRITE WAY TO GET RID OF ANGRY FEELINGS

Whenever You feel annoyed, frustrated, impatient, irritated, outraged, or resentful, write a letter to a person you would like to see or talk to.

State specifically,-- when, where, and what happened that caused you to feel Angry.

Use the word or words listed above that best describe your Angry Feelings.

I felt _____ when _____

_____

_____
_____
_____
_____
_____
_____

After writing your letter, tear it up and throw it away. The letter has served its purpose. You have gotten rid of your Angry Feelings and made room for Good Feelings and Pleasant Thoughts.

Writing out your Angry Feelings before going to sleep allows your Body and Mind to relax, rest comfortably, and recharge itself with Positive Energy. Regardless of the weather outside, you will rise and shine and be able to positively face the new day.

117

ACTIONS YOU CAN TAKE TO GET RID OF YOUR ANGRY FEELINGS

Take yourself to a quiet private place. You need space and time to cool down.

Take deep breaths.

Listen to soothing music.

Whistle or hum a favorite tune. Sing, dance, or play an instrument.

Read a book of jokes, puns, riddles, rhymes, tongue twisters.

Think of a funny situation that can bring on a smile or laugh.

Draw a picture.

Doodle cartoons. Use the circle shaped letters of the Alphabet -- a, c, d, g, o, p, q, u, y, to draw animals. Use curved, rounded shapes for features and facial expressions.

Look at pictures of favorite people and places.

Take a walk and enjoy the wonders of nature.

The Write Way to Help Worry,
Doubt and Fear to Disappear

Worry, Doubt, and Fear about future events cause one to ask "what if" questions.

Whenever You feel anxious, frightened, nervous, terrified, uptight, or worried about any future event, WRITE A WASTE LIST - A Worry, Anxiety, Stress and Tension List.

List all the "what if's" you are afraid will happen.

_____

_____

_____

_____

_____

_____

_____

_____

Write a reassuring response to your fearful "what if" questions.

Change the words "what if" " to "even if" and complete the following statement.

Even if_____

were to happen, I can handle it, because I believe that I can deal with whatever will happen.

State at least 2 steps you can take to handle the situation, should that event happen.

I can _____

_____

I can _____

_____

Place your LIST in an envelope. Store your LIST in a safe place.

Refer to the envelope whenever the event happens.

The Power of the Phrase "I Can Do It!!!"

Whenever You want Doubt and Fear to disappear, say the words "I can do it!" at least 5 times.

Increase your Voice Volume each time You say the Words.

Conclude by quickly raising your arm in mid-air, smiling, and uttering the word "yes"!!

Your Power is reinforced by the height of your arm movement and the broadness of your smile.

The Write Way to Relieve Sadness

Whenever You feel bored, confused, defeated, depressed, disappointed, discouraged, disgusted, downhearted, exhausted, lonely or unloved, write a letter to a person you would like to see or talk to.

Write about what makes You feel Sad. Use the word or words listed above that best describe your Feelings.

I feel_____
when I remember (state when, where, and what happened)

_____
_____
_____
_____
_____
_____
_____
_____
_____
_____
_____
_____
_____
_____
_____
_____
_____
_____
_____

_____

Your letter does not require mailing. The letter has served its purpose.

You have gotten rid of your Sad Feelings and made room for Good Feelings and Pleasant Thoughts.

Your Brain --- A Powerful Personal Computer

Everyone is born with a Personal Computer that never sleeps --a Brain.

For your entire Lifetime, your Brain is the Processing Center for all your Knowledge and Experiences.

All information concerning what you hear, see, smell, taste, and touch is stored in your Brain's Memory Data Bank.

The information in your Memory Data Bank is stored and filed into either a Positive Energy Program or a Negative Energy Program.

The Positive Energy Program stores the Positive Thoughts and the Good Feelings of Joy, Love, and Hope.

The Negative Energy Program stores the Angry, Anxious, Sad Feelings and Thoughts.

You are the Programmer. Each day you have a choice -- to use the Positive Energy Program or the Negative Energy Program.

The Program you choose to use will determine the kind of day you will have.

To Have A Good Day, choose to Accentuate The Positive and Eliminate The Negative!!!

Choices – Choices – and More Choices

From the minute you get up to the minute you go to sleep, you are constantly making many choices.

Do I choose to wake up early or late?

What color and kind of clothes do I choose to wear?

How do I choose to comb my hair?

Do I choose to have long or short hair?

What books, magazines, papers do I choose to read?

What TV shows do I choose to watch?

What games do I choose to play?

What kind of music do I choose to listen to?

What kind of friends do I choose to have?

How do I choose to feel about attending school?

How well do I choose to listen to my parents, teachers, others?

How well do I choose to concentrate?

Whom do I choose to talk to when I have a problem?

How do I choose to feel and act when I make a mistake?

How do I choose to handle my Feelings when I am Angry, Frustrated or Worried?

What do I choose to eat and drink for breakfast, lunch, dinner, and snacktime?

You are responsible for all the Choices you make in your Lifetime.

Your Choices influence all your Life Experiences and determine how well you will function.

Your Choices trigger, change, and set in motion Positive or Negative Thoughts.

Your Good Choices trigger your Positive Thoughts.

Your Positive Thoughts form your Positive Belief System.

Your Positive Belief System influences your Attitudes and your Behavior.

CHOOSE TO MAKE GOOD CHOICES!
Choice Statements to Trigger Positive Thoughts

Choose one or more Statements that are meaningful for you.

Write, Read, and Say your Choice Statements every day for a minimum of 30 consecutive days. It takes a minimum of 30 consecutive days of practice to successfully program a new Habit into your Memory Data Bank.

I choose to have a strong Positive Belief System.

I choose to feel happy.

I choose to enjoy every day.

I choose to smile at least 3 times a day.

I choose to be responsible for my Choices, Thoughts, and Actions.

I choose to do what it takes to have a healthy, highly efficient Body and Mind.

I choose to be aware of any substances, stimuli, or toxins that affect my Body Chemistry and impair my Immune System.

I choose to control whatever I put into my mouth.

I choose to believe I can succeed.

I choose to have a Good Day - Every Day.

POSITIVE CHOICES ARE THE KEY TO SUCCESS!

Choose to Have Super Habits

When you repeatedly practice doing something a certain way, you form a Habit.

The more you reinforce, or use the Habit, the stronger it becomes.

Strong Habits become a part of your Automatic Behavior System.

You no longer have to think about how the action is to be done. You just spontaneously do it.

Habits that you have stored in your Automatic Behavior System are: eating, sleeping, talking, walking, running, jumping, playing, skipping, dressing, routines that you follow to take care of your physical needs.

As you continue to learn, you constantly develop more Skills and Habits.

Super Habits allow your Body Systems to function with maximum efficiency.

Choose to have an Automatic Behavior System filled with Super Habits.

CHOOSE TO BE THE BEST YOU CAN BE!!!

Your Brain - your Personal Computer - is designed to process one new Habit at a time. Trying to form more than one new Habit at any one time, confuses your Brain.

It takes time to form a Habit. The length of time to learn a new Habit varies for each Person. For some, it may be a month. For some, it may be several months.

C P R Formula for Programming Super Habits into Your Memory Data Bank.

Commitment + Consistency + Patience + Practice + Repetition + Reinforcement

It Does Matter How and Where You Cross Your 't's"!!!

You are only a line away from having Self-Confidence and Strong Will Power.

"t-bars" that are long, strong, evenly balanced and placed close to the top of the "t-stem," show and tell that the Writer has Self-Confidence, High Self Esteem, sets achievable Goals, and has the Power to overcome everyday obstacles.

WILLPOWER TRANSLATES WISHES INTO ACTION !!!

The Write Way to Raise Your Level of Confidence and Willpower

Use 8 1/2 size paper.

Practice writing the Key Words and Sentences for 20 minutes a day for 30 consecutive days. It takes a minimum of 30 days to Program a new Habit into your Memory Data Bank.

After each Practice Session, check for accuracy of the "t-bar" placement.

Successful Programming into your Memory Data Bank requires a minimum of <u>30 consecutive accurate entries,</u>

<u>NOTE:</u>

It takes Time to form new Habits.

The length of Time to learn a new Habit varies for each Person.

For some, it may be a month. For some, it may be several months.

KEY WORDS FOR SUCCESSFUL PROGRAMMING: CONSISTENCY -- PATIENCE – REPETITION (CPR)

The Write Way to "t-bars" That Show and Tell
Self-Confidence and Willpower

Long, strong, evenly balanced "t-bars" are placed
close to the top of the "t-stem"

KEY WORDS
triumph
strength
trust
time

KEY STATEMENTS
I take the time to set realistic goals.
I take the time to appreciate my achievements.
I take the time to do my best.
I trust in my strength and ability to triumph.
I feel great about me.
I have strong faith and belief in myself.

The Write Way to Be the "I" You Want to Be

You are what you feel.   I feel that I am a winner!

You believe what you feel.   I believe that I am a winner!

You are what you believe.   I am a winner!

From the <u>Glossary Of Positive Adjectives</u>, choose 5 positive adjectives that describe the " I " you want to be.

For each word selected, complete the following 3 statements.
I feel that I am _____.
I believe that I am _____.
I am _____.

Write and say each set of 3 statements, 3 times each, every day for at least 30 consecutive days.

Say the Statements to yourself any time you want to Feel Good about Yourself.

It takes at least 30 consecutive days to successfully program your Positive Statements into your Memory Data Bank.

After 30 consecutive days, select another 5 adjectives and repeat the Programming Process. There is no limit to the number of adjectives that you may wish to include in your Belief System.

YOU ARE WHO YOU BELIEVE YOU ARE !!!

Reminder:
It makes a difference where and how you cross your "t-bars".

Place the long, strong, evenly balanced "t-bar" close to the top of the "t-stem"

Glossary of Positive Adjectives

A --- agreeable, alert, ambitious, amiable
B --- brainy, brave, bright, brilliant
C --- capable, caring, charitable, charming, cheerful, competent, conscientious, cooperative
D --- dedicated, delightful, dynamic
E --- enthusiastic
F --- faithful, friendly
G --- generous, gentle, great
H --- helpful, healthy, honorable
I --- inquisitive, intelligent, interesting
J --- jolly, jovial, joyful, jubilant
K --- knowledgeable
L --- lively, lovable, loyal
M --- marvelous, mighty, mild-mannered, moral
N --- neat, neighborly
O --- outstanding
P --- patient, pleasant, polite
R --- reasonable, receptive, respectful, responsible
S --- satisfied, successful
T --- talented, thoughtful, tolerant, trustworthy, truthful
U --- understanding, unique, unselfish
V --- vibrant, victorious, vigorous, vivacious
W --- willing, witty, wonderful

Positive Descriptive Name Profiles

How do You view Yourself?

Create your own Positive Descriptive Name Profile.

Write the letters of your Name in a vertical line.

Select one or more Positive Adjectives that begin with each letter in your Name and that seem to describe you.

Use <u>The Glossary Of Positive Adjectives</u> to help you with your selections.

How do Others view You?

Ask Others to create a Positive Descriptive Profile for your Name.

Do other People see you in the same way as you see yourself? Are you viewed differently by different people?

How do You view Others?

Create Positive Descriptive Name Profiles for People you know. Send Positive Name Profile cards to your Favorite Persons

Fun activity in a Group Setting -- "Guess Who?"

Each Person in the Group receives a slip of paper with the Name of a Group Member written on it.

A Profile is to be created for the Name.

The slip is then folded and placed in a container.

Each Person takes a folded slip from the container and reads the adjectives aloud, without revealing the Name.

The Group Members are to guess who fits the description.

Extended Version of "Guess Who?" -- Rounds of Name Profiles

Each Person receives a slip of paper with the same Person's Name written on it.

The Name Profile is to be written on the other side of the paper.

After completing the Profile, the slip is folded, revealing only the Name of the individual.

The papers are placed in a container.

The number of People participating in the activity determines the number of rounds.

The rounds continue until each Person has been Profiled by all participants.

The Profiles are then distributed to the rightful owners.

Each Person has a collection of his/her own Name Profiles.

Each Person has the option of sharing the Profiles with the Group.

In how many different ways is one Person viewed?

Pointer–Cise to Positively Energize

A simple exercise routine that is guaranteed to generate physical and emotional fitness, flexibility, balance, and high Self-Esteem.

A physical examination is not required prior to Pointer-cising. There are no physical restrictions, limitations, side effects, or risks.

When?

The number and length of daily sessions depends upon your need throughout each day.

Where?

Pointer-cising can be done in a standing, sitting, or reclining position. Your comfort is the determining factor.

What equipment is needed?

Your favored Pointer Finger, of either your right or left hand.

Pointer-cising Routine

1. Select one or more Statements from "I" Statements For Positive Energy Power.

2. Bend your elbow and face the palm side of your hand.

3. Straighten your Pointer Finger. Relax all other fingers.

4. Each Statement begins with the Letter "I" Your straight Pointer represents that word.

5. Bend your Pointer Finger and point to yourself as you say the remaining words in the Statement.

6. Return Pointer to a straight position at the end of the Statement.

Choose to say as many Statements as many times as you wish.

Repeat steps 2- 6 each time you say a Statement.

For added fun, and pleasure when Pointer-cising

- Draw a smile on your Pointer. (2 dots and a curve)
- Place a Smile Sticker on your Pointer.
- Say your "I" Statements in front of a mirror.
- Add "yes" or "yes, I believe" before each statement.
- Smile and nod your head up and down. Avoid any side to side motion.
- End each Statement with a "thumbs up" signal.

Important Reminder:

Your Pointer always faces you and bends only in your direction.

Do not use the Pointer in an outward direction. That accusing, blaming motion depletes your Positive Energy Power!!! (PEP)

"I" Statements for Positive Energy Power

I am the only one who is responsible for my thoughts and behavior.

I am responsible for my reactions to circumstances.

I am honest and open with myself.

I am discovering what it takes for me to feel good.

I am proud of myself.

I am at peace with myself.

I am comfortable with myself.

I am a kind and caring person.

I am consistent.

I am decisive.

I am a good listener.

I am in control of what passes my lips-- food going in and words coming out.

I accept myself for who I am.

I aim to be the best that I can be.

I appreciate all the good things that I can do.

I appreciate my uniqueness.

I believe in myself.

I believe that I have the courage and inner strength to get through difficult times.

I believe that I am an important Individual.

I believe that I count.

I believe that I am a Winner.

I believe that I am a good and deserving person.

I believe that I am a Success.

I believe that I can do anything that I make up my mind to do.

I believe that I have the power to solve my problems.

I have faith in my ability to achieve.

I hold no grudges.

I learn and grow from my mistakes.

I like who I am.

I respect myself.

I trust myself.

I value myself.

The Comfort of a Hug – A Simple Pain-Free Workout

A HUG is an important source of Comfort.

Aches and Pains need the Comfort of a Hug.

When you give and get a Hug, you establish a reciprocal flow of positive energy. By extending your arms, you instantly release Muscle Tension.

Give and get at least one Hug each day.

If no one is available, Hug yourself.

PICTURE VISUALIZATION

Enjoy the Spring Season all year round.

Surround yourself with pictures, posters, or paintings of scenes that celebrate Spring -- the Season of Renewal, Harmony, Peace, Hope, and Joy.

Visualize yourself within the setting.

Observe the Colors. Listen to the Sounds. Smell the Scents.

For Pleasant Dreams, view the picture/ poster before going to sleep.

To have a great day, view the picture /poster upon waking.

How Do You Feel About Your Mistakes?

You make a mistake towards the end of your writing page.
Do you react by:
- becoming annoyed, angry, frustrated, tense?
- grabbing an eraser, vigorously rubbing out the mistake and only succeed in making a dark mark?
- crumbling the paper into a ball and throwing it onto the floor?
- becoming very annoyed because you are starting all over again?
- calling yourself "stupid", "dumb", "moron", "idiot"?

You fail a test.
Do you react by:
- feeling annoyed, angry, frustrated, embarrassed, worried, ashamed?
- yelling, screaming, and stamping your feet?
- getting into an argument with the first person you see?
- hitting the closest thing you see?
- thinking:
I can't do anything right.
I'll never be able to learn.
I'm just doomed to fail.
It's too hard.
What's the use?
I'll never pass my test.
Who cares, anyway?
I don't care what happens.
I'd rather have fun and not think about it.
It's all the teacher's fault.

If you answered "yes" to any of these negative reactions, you are stuck in a destructive Negative Belief Program.

Your Negative Feelings are not allowing you to focus in on your problem.

Your mistakes and failures are really telling you that you have a weakness in that area.

You have not really understood the information. You have not spent sufficient time learning the information. You have not concentrated well enough.

It is time to take Positive Action.

Program these thoughts into your Memory Data Bank.

Human beings are not perfect. Human beings do make mistakes.

Mistakes are stepping stones to success. I learn and grow from my mistakes.

It's okay to ask for help when I don't understand something.

I can schedule sufficient time for effective study.

I can pass my tests.

I can succeed.

BELIEVE YOU CAN SUCCEED AND YOU WILL!!!

The Power of Journaling

Start a journal of "Happy Moments"
Make daily entries.
Date each entry.

Write about one or more events that made you feel that you had a Great Day.

Indicate specifically - when, where, and what happened.

Writing in your journal before going to sleep is a relaxing activity and is the right way to go for pleasant dreams.

Read your Journal whenever you want to refresh your Memory and relive happy, exciting events. It's guaranteed to keep you smiling.

Share your journal of "Happy Moments" with others.

The Power of Smiles and Laughter

Laughter is the most inexpensive and most effective wonder drug.

Laughter is a universal medicine.

Bertrand Russell

A Mile Of Smiles Each Day Goes A Long Way To Heal What Ails You.

Relaxes your Facial Muscles.

Softens your Frown Lines.

Acts as a Natural Face Lift.

A Laugh A Day Keeps The Stress Away.

Gives your Heart and Diaphragm Muscles a beneficial workout.

Improves your Circulation.

Fills your Lungs with Oxygen-rich air.

Clears your Respiratory Passages.

Stimulates the release of Endorphins into your Bloodstream.

Endorphins are Hormones that help you to "feel good".

Reduces the tension in your Central Nervous System.

Laughter is free, legal, has no calories, no cholesterol, no preservatives, no artificial ingredients and is absolutely safe.

Dale Irvin

Alpha Word Collections – The Write Way to Miles of Smiles and Tons of Tongue Twisters

An ALPHA WORD COLLECTION is made up of NOUNS, ADJECTIVES, and ACTION WORDS that start with the same Letter of the Alphabet.

For tons of Tongue Twisters
Select one or more Nouns.
Add one or more Adjectives that describe the Nouns.
Add one or more Action Words that tell what the Noun or Nouns are doing.
Say your completed Sentences out loud, 3 or more times.
Share your Tongue Twisters with others.

Start an Alpha Word Collection of Nouns, Adjectives, and Action Words for every letter of the Alphabet.

To expand the supply of Words for your Tongue Twisters, select and combine Nouns, Adjectives, and Action Words from any Alpha Word Collection.

Note:
A Dictionary is the source to use to help your Word Collection grow.

The "a" Word Collection of Nouns, Adjectives, and Action Words

aims at adding an abundance of Tongue Twisters

NOUNS
accident, ache, agreement, air, airplane, airport,
alarm, alligator, allowance, army, animal, ant, ape,
apple, apron, aquarium, area, adventure, ax,
arm, aunt, athlete, attachment, attention, attitude,
autumn, award, abundance.
Alice, Andrea, Anne, Alyson, Adeline, Amanda, Aileen,
Anita, Agatha, Amy, Ariel, Annette, Arlene, Alexandra,
Aaron, Adam, Alvin, Albert, Anthony, Andrew, Arthur,
Adrian, Althea, Allen, Alex.

DESCRIPTIVE WORDS
able, abundant, adorable, affectionate, aggressive,
agreeable, alert, amused, angry, active, ambitious,
Amiable, anxious, atrocious, attentive, attractive,
awkward, awful, athletic, atrocious, automatic

ACTION WORDS
act, add, admire, agree, aim, allow, alter, answer,
appear, are, arrive, ask, attach, attack, avoid, awake,
ate, approve, assist, appreciate.

Examples:
The active alligator appeared at the airy airport.
The amiable ape ate an abundance of awful apples.

The "d" Word Collection of
Nouns, Adjectives, and Action Words

definitely does deliver dozens of Tongue Twisters

Nouns
dad, dance, danger, date, dateline, daughter, day
decision, decoration, deed, deer, degree, dentist, desk,
diamond, digit, dime, dinner, dinosaur, direction,
directory, dirt, disappearance, discussion, disk, dog,
doctor, doll, dollar, dollhouse, donkey, door, dot,
dragon, dream, dress, drum, duck, dude, dust,
Diane, Dale, Doris, Donna, Daphne, Doreen, Danielle,
Dolores, Dana, Deborah, Deanna, Daniel, Dennis, Donald,
Douglas, Drew, David

Descriptive Words
dangerous, daring, dark, deafening, defiant, delicious
delighted, dense, desperate, determined, devoted,
difficult, dim, dirty, disagreeable, discouraged, disgusted,
disliked, dissatisfied, distant, distinct, doubtful, dozen,
downhearted, downstairs, dreadful, dreary, dry,
dull, durable, dusk, dusty, dynamic

Action Words
dance, dangle, dare, dash, decide, decorate, deliver,
demand, deny, describe, deserve, destroy, do, does, did,
die, dig, digest, disappear, discuss, dismiss, drink, draw,
drive, drop, drown, dump

Examples:
The determined dog dug dozens of deep, dark ditches.
The dynamic dragon danced with the delighted dinosaur.

The "g" Word Collection
of Nouns, Adjectives, and Action Words

gives you great Tongue Twisters

Nouns
gadget, gallon, game, gang, gap, garage, garden,
gas, gate, geese, gift, giraffe, girl, gland, glare,
glass, globe, glove, glue, goal, goat, goldfish, goose,
gown, grade, graduate, grain, grandmother, grandfather,
grape, grass, grease, ground, group, guide, gum, gun,
Gail, Greta, Grace, Gladys, Gina, Gloria, Gwen,
George, Gary, Gregory, Gerard, Gerald, Gabriel

Descriptive Words
generous, gentle, genuine, gigantic glad, glamorous,
gleaming, glistening, gloomy, glorious, glossy, glowing,
glum, golden, good, good-natured, graceful, gracious,
grainy, grand, grateful, gray, greasy, great, green,
grim, grotesque, guilty

Action Words
gain, gallop, gather, get, give, glare, glide, glisten, glow,
go, graduate, grant, grill, grind, groan, grow, growl

Examples:
The gigantic giraffe galloped to the green, glossy grass.
Gary gave Grace a graceful, golden goose.

The "l" Word Collection
of Nouns, Adjectives, and Action Words

leads to lively Tongue Twisters

Nouns
ladder, lady, lake, lamb, lamp, land, law, leaf, leaflet,
leak, leopard, leash, leather, leg, lemon, lemonade,
length, lens, letter, library, lid, life, light, lime, line,
lion, lip, list, lizard, loaf, lock, log, lunch,
Lisa, Laura, Lillian, Lenore, Lauren, Linda, Lesley,
Lindsay, Louise, Leon, Larry, Leonard, Leo, Luke,
Louis, Lyle, Lorraine, Lila

Descriptive Words
large, last, late, lazy, least, left, light, little, lively,
lonely, lonesome, long, loose, lost, loud, lovable,
low, lucky

Action Words
laugh, lean, learn, leap, leave, let, lift, listen, live, look,
lose, lead

Examples:
The little lizard and the large leopard like lamb for lunch.
Larry and Lisa lost the last, long, legal letter.

The "m" Word Collection of
Nouns, Adjectives, and Action Words

makes for many, merry Tongue Twisters

Nouns
machine, mail, man, map, mark, mat, match,
material, meal, meat, medicine, men, mice,
mile, milk, minute, mistake, moment, money,
monkey, month, morning, mother, mountain, mouse, mouth,
mud, murmur, music, muzzle, Max, Martin, Matthew, Mark,
Margaret, Megan, Minerva, Melanie, Mitchell, Marvin,
Marilyn, Michelle, Millicent, Madeline

Descriptive Words
magic, magnificent, many, marvelous, massive,
meager, mean, meek, merry, metallic, microscopic,
mighty, mild, million, miniature, miserable, misty,
modern, moody, motionless, muddy

Action Words
made, march, marry, may, meet,
melt, miss, move, murmur

Examples:
The many, mighty men marched many muddy miles.
Many merry monkeys made merry music.

The "t" Word Collection of
Nouns, Adjectives, and Action Words

tend to lead to tons of Tongue Twisters

Nouns
table, tag, tail, tailor, tale, tank, tape, tax, taxi,
tea, teacup, teacher, team, teenager, teaspoon, teeth,
telegram, telephone, temperature, temple, tenant, tennis,
tent, terrier, test, textbook, thief, thimble, thorn,
thought, thread, throat, throne, thumb, thunder, ticket,
tie, tiger, time, timetable, tire, title, toad, toast,
tobacco, toes, tomato, ton, tongue, tools, tooth, toothache,
toothbrush, top, tortoise, total, towel, town, toys, track,
traffic, trailer, trail, train, transfer, trap, trash,
traveler, tray, treat, treatment, treasure, tree, trial,
triangle, tribe, trick, tricycle, trip, trouble, truck,
trumpet, trunk, truth, tub, tube, tunnel, turkey, turn,
turtle, turnpike, tusks, twig, twin, twine, typewriter,
tyrannosaurus
Thomas, Terry, Tina, Timothy, Theresa, Theodore,
Thelma

Descriptive Words
talkative, tall, tame, tan, tasteless, tasty, tearful,
temporary, ten, tender, tense, terrible, terrific, terrified,
the, their, these, thick, thin, third, thirsty, thirteen,
thirty, this, those, thoughtful, thousand, three,
thousandth, thrilled, thunderous, tidy, tight, timid,
tiny, tired, tolerant, tough, towering, tragic, trivial,
tremendous, triumphant, troubled, trustworthy, truthful,
twelve, twelfth, twentieth, twenty two

Action Words
take, talk, tangle, tap, tape, taste, teach, tear, tease,
tell, test ,thank ,think, throw, thump, tickle, tie,
toss, touch, train, transfer, treasure, travel ,treat,
tremble, trip, trim, trust, try, tumble, turn, twist

Examples:
Thirty-two teenagers took ten tough tests.
Ten tigers took turns talking to twenty-two trembling terriers.
Smiles and Laughter are meant to be shared.

Highly Recommended -- THE HEALTHY HUMOR PROJECT

Write and Self-Publish an annual edition of <u>LAUGH YOUR WAY TO GOOD HEALTH</u>, a Collection of Tongue Twisters, Rhymes, and Riddles.

Share your Book with Children in Hospitals. It is guaranteed to help them to heal!!!

Acts of Kindness – A Positive Energy Project

Reach out and Help Others. Say a Kind Word. Perform a Kind Deed.

Kind Words, Compliments, and Compassion can instantly increase the Positive Energy Power (PEP) of the Giver and the Receiver.

Invite Relatives, Friends, and Classmates to participate in the Acts of Kindness Project.

Keep a Daily Score of Credits Earned.

Earn 2 credits for each time you do an Act of Kindness, Share a Smile, Hug Someone, Extend a Helping Hand, Use the magic words Please "and "Thank You." The Person with the highest Weekly Score becomes the Winner of the Week.

Form a Committee to decide what kind of Recognition, Rewards, or Awards will give pleasure to the Weekly Winners with the highest scores.

Share the results of your Acts of Kindness Project with other Classes, Schools, Organizations, and the News Media.

Enjoy Your Positive Energy Power !!!

What You Eat Affects How You Feel

Your Mind and Body need Energy in order to function.

Feelings provide the Emotional Energy for your Mind.

Food provides the Chemical Energy for your Body.

Food is made up of Chemicals called Nutrients. Nutrients are Proteins, Complex Carbohydrates, Essential Fats, Vitamins, and Minerals.

Every bite of Food that passes your Lips, causes a chemical reaction within your Body.

Your Body's Digestive System is designed to chemically simplify Proteins, Complex Carbohydrates, and Essential Fats in order to provide the Chemical Energy that will satisfy your unique Daily Body Requirements for Optimum Performance.

It is necessary to have a Balance of both Protein and Complex Carbohydrates.

Proteins and Complex Carbohydrates interact in order to maintain a steady Blood Sugar Level.

Food sources for Protein

Foods of animal origin: lean meat, poultry, seafood, eggs, non-fat milk, cheese

Vegetable sources of Protein: beans, brown rice, grains, lentils, peas, plain non-fat yogurt, seeds, soybean products, tofu, unsalted raw nuts, whole grain cereals, wheat germ.

Food sources for Complex Carbohydrates: barley, beans, buckwheat, corn, nuts, fresh fruits, leafy vegetables, legumes, natural whole grains, millet, oats, rye, wheat.

Food sources for Essential Fatty Acids: avocados, nuts, seeds, soybeans, wheat germ, cold water fish oils - mackerel, salmon, sardines, vegetable oils - canola, olive, safflower, sesame.

Important To Note:

Poor nutritional habits can contribute to dizziness, allergies, headaches, memory problems.

Your Memory and Blood Sugar Level are negatively affected when you skip breakfast.

The Color of the Foods That You Eat Affects How You Feel

For Sustained Optimum Energy, select Red, Orange, Yellow Foods for your Breakfast.

For a Relaxed Nervous System, select Green Vegetables and Salads as part of your Evening Meal. A relaxed Nervous System prepares your Body for restful sleep -- the time needed for internal repair of Cells and Body Tissues so that you have renewed Energy in the morning.

A FOOD PALETTE FOR YOUR PALATE

Use the Food Palette to select the Foods that will provide the Energy that your Body needs for Daily Optimum Functioning.

Red Foods -- rich in all B Vitamins -- provide strong vitalizing Physical Energy.

Orange Foods -- rich in Vitamins A, B, C -- stimulate Physical Vitality and a Feeling of Well-Being.

Yellow Foods rich in Vitamins A, C -- stimulate the Metabolism.

Green Foods rich in Vitamin C and Minerals -- stimulate the Nerves, relax and refresh the Body.

Blue and Purple Foods calm the Emotions.

Red Foods: beets, tomatoes, radishes, red cabbage, red beans, black cherries, red currants, red plums, red grapes, raspberries, strawberries, watermelon, apples

Orange Foods: carrots, sweet potatoes, squash, pumpkins peaches, apricots, cantaloupes, oranges, tangerines, nectarines, mangoes, papaya, persimmons eggs, cheese

Yellow Foods: corn, yellow sweet potatoes, yellow peppers, yellow squash, parsnips bananas, pineapples, lemons, grapefruit, figs, peaches, honeydew melons eggs, butter, yellow cheese, mustard

Green Foods: green beans, green peas, spinach, asparagus, cabbage, zucchini, green peppers, broccoli, cucumbers, avocado, green celery, raw green salads, parsley, olives

Blue Foods blueberries, blue plums,

Purple Foods: purple   broccoli,   beet   tops,   eggplant, blackberries, prunes

LISTEN TO YOUR BODY SIGNALS

Your Body is a wonderful complex structure with an amazing power to heal itself.

Your Body needs your cooperation in order to function effectively and efficiently.

Your Body is constantly sending you signals.

Your Body lets you know when it needs nutritional energy. Signal is feeling of hunger.

Your Body lets you know when it is time for cell repair and revitalization.

Signal is fatigue and drowsiness.

Your Body lets you know when something is wrong - an imbalance, a deficiency or weakness exists.

Signal is pain and discomfort.

Failure to listen to your Body signals interferes with the state of your Health. Your Body becomes "run down". Pain increases in severity. The condition can become chronic.

Take Good Care Of The One Body That You Have For A Lifetime !!!

THE POWERFUL YOU

Your Feelings and Thoughts provide the Emotional Energy for your Mind.

You are in charge of your Feelings and Thoughts.

Choose to have Positive Thoughts. Positive Thoughts give you a Sense of Well- Being.

Your Food Choices provide the Chemical Energy for your Body's needs.

You control what substances will pass through your Lips and enter your Body. Your Lips follow your orders. They open with your approval. They remain closed until they get your approval.

Choose Foods that will provide optimum Chemical Energy, boost your Immune System and reduce Emotional Stress.

What You choose to eat determines how well You Feel, Think, and Perform !!!

One More Try Can Do It!!!

When You think that You have had it, and are ready to give up and pack it in

Try one more time.

When You are sure that You will never succeed

Try one more time.

When You think it is impossible, too hard to do, and it will never work

Try one more time.

When You think that it will never happen

Try one more time.

When You think that all is lost and it will never get better

Try one more time.

When You think that You have reached the end of your rope and there is no place to turn

Try one more time.

When You think that You will never win

Try one more time.

If You Don't Try One More Time, You Will Never Know If You Might Have Won!!!

APPENDIX

GRAPHOLOGY - THE SCIENTIFIC STUDY OF HANDWRITING ANALYSIS

BASIC CONCEPTS OF GRAPHOLOGY PRESENTED IN A SIMPLIFIED CAPSULE FORM

THE SCIENCE OF GRAPHOLOGY: A BRIEF HISTORY

Graphology is a reliable, unbiased scientific system of Personality Assessment through the study of a Person's Handwriting.

Graphology is not a new science.

The Chinese noted a relationship between Handwriting, Character, and Personality as early as the 11th century.

In 1622, Camillo Baldi, Doctor and Professor at the University of Bologna, wrote the oldest published book on the subject of Graphology. *How To judge The Nature and The Character of a Person From His Letter.*

Ideographia by Alderisius Prosper, published in Bologna in the beginning of the 17th century, identified the relationship between Handwriting Traits and Character Traits.

In the 1870's, French Priests, Abbe Flandria, and Abbe Jean-Hypolyte Michon (known as the Founder of European Graphology) published writing in which they referred to Graphology as the art of knowing men by their Handwriting.

Ludwig Klages, well-known German Philosopher, established Laws and Principles of Graphology during the late 1800s and early 1900s.

Sigmund Freud published information about the validity and use of Graphology.

Alfred Binet, Inventor of the IQ test, referred to Graphology as " the Science of the Future".

Milton Bunker, in his intensive, methodical research from 1915 - 1929, discovered the importance of the Handwriting Stroke, identified over 100 Personality Traits in Handwriting, and founded the International Graphoanalysis Society and School in Chicago, Illinois.

The Research Behind The Concept: An Individual's Personality Traits Can Be Changed By Changing The Individual's Handwriting.

Between 1929 and 1931, The Concept was clinically tested at the Sorbonne by French psychologist Professor Charles Henry and physician Dr. Pierre Janet. The results achieved were positive and impressive.

In 1931, Dr. Pierre Menard, a distinguished psychology professor, lecturer, and author of many books and articles on Medicine and Psychology, put the tested Concept into practice. His success in positively modifying children's behavior by changing their handwriting won the support of doctors, psychologists, and teachers.

Based upon 25 years of extensive research, noted Graphologist, Paul de Sainte Columbe, in his book *Grapho-Therapeuties* published in 1966, claimed success in using handwriting changes to bring about personality improvements.

Dr. Richard J. Stoller, in his book, <u>Write Right: Change Your Writing to Change Your Life</u>, published in 1977, showed that, by incorporating positive trait strokes into a child's handwriting, negative attitudes and a poor self-image can be changed. The Concept, used in both individual and group settings, proved to be effective in approximately 80% of the cases.

Graphology Today

In France, England, Germany, Switzerland, Holland, Canada, South America, and the United States, Handwriting Analysts are making significant contributions in the areas of Personnel Selection and Management Screening, Medicine, Psychiatry, Sociology, Criminology, Education, and Marriage/Compatibility Counseling.

In Courtrooms around the World, the testimony of Handwriting Experts is used to determine whether an Individual is capable of committing a particular type of crime.

Graphology cannot determine an Individual's age, race, sex, or marital status.

Graphology can, however, serve as a reliable, unbiased, and non-judgmental tool to identify an Individual's Personality Strengths, Thinking Patterns, and Emotional State of Mind at the time the graphic symbols are placed on the paper.

Graphology is indeed an exciting Science that points the way to Understanding, Insight, Growth, and Change.

Fascinating Handwriting Facts

Regardless of the Writing Style that has been learned, each Individual develops his/her own unique Writing Style that is as identifiable as his/her fingerprints.

It has been noted that the chances of 2 Individuals having Identical Writing Patterns is 1 in 68 trillion.

Chemical sensitivities, allergies, drugs, alcohol, medications, illness, and fatigue can alter an Individual's Handwriting. Changes in Pressure, and in Letter Size and Shape, can be noted within 20 minutes after an allergic substance has entered the Body.

The Grapho Trait Detectors That Show and Tell a Writer's Personality Traits and Emotional State of Mind at the Time the Symbols are Placed on the Paper

Slant

Pressure

Letter Size

Baseline

Does Your "Slant On life" Tend To Lean To The Right Or To The Left?
Do You Tend To Look Forward To The Future Or Look Back On The Past?

The Handwriting Slant reflects a Writer's Temperament and Emotional Response to environment, people, and the future.
The Handwriting Slant can lean to the right, left, or stand straight up and down.

A Moderate Rightward Slant shows and tells that the Writer is an Extrovert - outgoing, friendly, sociable, affectionate, future-oriented and eagerly anticipates events to come.

A Vertical Slant that stands straight up and down, shows and tells that the Writer is Level-Headed, sensible, logical, realistic, reserved, independent, analytical, and focuses on issues in the present time.

A Leftward Slant shows and tells that the Writer is an Introvert - self-oriented, reserved, impersonal, undemonstrative, resistant to change, withdraws from social interaction, has difficulty expressing his/her feelings, and seeks emotional security by retreating into the past.

SLANT DIAGRAM

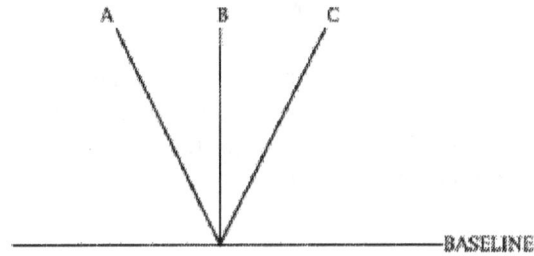

A -- Left Slant Leans Back To The Left.
B -- Vertical Slant Stands Straight Up And Down.
C -- Right Slant Leans Forward To The Right.

LEFT SLANT   VERTICAL SLANT   RIGHT SLANT

LEFT SLANT   VERTICAL SLANT   RIGHT SLANT

Pen Pressure can determine a Writer's Level of Energy, Vitality and Determination.

How lightly or heavily a Writer presses on a ball point pen, at the time of writing, reveals his/her vitality, will power, health and emotional intensity.

Moderately Heavy Pressure, represented by firm, dark, thick pen strokes, shows and tells that the Writer is energetic, ambitious, assertive, determined, has a retentive memory, and is in good physical health.

Light Pressure, represented by fine, thin, light, pen strokes, shows and tells that the Writer is gentle, calm, passive, sensitive, impressionable, easily influenced, lacks physical energy, determination and confidence, resists commitments, easily forgets and forgives.

One Size Does Not Fit All!

A Writer's Letter Size can be Large, Moderate, or Small.
A Writer's Letter Size shows and tells how a Writer relates to his/her environment and his/her capacity for concentration.

A Large Letter Size shows and tells that the Writer
-- is extroverted, people and action oriented, outgoing, outspoken, and energetic.
-- has a need to be noticed.
-- seeks recognition and approval of others.
-- is concerned with generalities rather than specifics.
-- is unwilling to concentrate on small details or be confined to a limited are of space.

A Moderate Letter Size shows and tells that the Writer
-- is practical, realistic, reliable, adaptable, socially well-balanced.
-- has average ability to concentrate.

A Small Letter Size shows and tells that the Writer

-- is introverted, modest, analytical, precise, attentive to details, and not too communicative.

-- has a high level of concentration, concentrates on one thing at a time.

-- avoids close relationships.

Interesting Note:

When you increase your concentration, your writing simultaneously becomes smaller.

When you are tired of writing, you lose your ability to concentrate, and your writing becomes larger.

The Baseline - The Line of Reality

The Baseline is the Line formed when writing on a blank piece of paper.

The Baseline shows and tells a Writer's Mood, and Attitude in dealing with the events in his/her Life.

The Baseline Direction may go uphill, downhill, or remain level. You can identify a Rising, Descending or Level Baseline Direction, by following the direction of the 1st word to the last word on a Line of Writing, Hold the ruler so that it is parallel to the bottom of the page. Place the ruler under the first word on the Writing Line and see the Direction that the last word takes on the Writing Line. Is it uphill, downhill, or level?

The Baseline Direction can vary from line to line. Moods constantly fluctuate.

The Baseline Direction reflects Mood Changes.

A Level Baseline Direction shows and tells that the Writer is reliable, realistic, even tempered, and level-headed.

A slightly Bouncy Baseline Direction shows and tells that the Writer is flexible, lively, and is feeling happy.

An Ascending, Rising Baseline Direction shows and tells that the Writer is feeling energetic, optimistic, enthusiastic, joyful, and ambitious.

A Descending, Downward Baseline Direction shows and tells that the Writer is feeling depressed, discouraged, disillusioned, fatigued, unhappy, or ill.

The Write Way to Tell if You Are Feeling Optimistic or Pessimistic

Quickly read the following message.

Hope is nowhere.

Place the message aside. Without looking at it, record what you read on an unlined sheet of paper, (Do not print.)

About the Hope message.

If you read and recorded the message as: Hope is nowhere, at the moment you are feeling Pessimistic.

if you read and recorded the message as: Hope is now here, at the moment you are feeling Optimistic.

Place a ruler at the Baseline of your written message.

An upward slanted Baseline shows and tells that at the moment you are feeling Optimistic.

A downward slanted Baseline shows and tells that at the moment you are feeling Pessimistic.

To boost your level of Enthusiasm, practice writing t-bars that are long, strong, evenly balanced, placed close to the top of the t-stem and slanted upwards.

HOPE IS A STRONG BELIEF IN A DESIRED OUTCOME.

HOPE stands for

H   Health, Happiness
O   Optimism, Open-mindedness
P   Patience, Peace of Mind
E   Enthusiasm, Encouragement

ALWAYS HAVE HOPE!!

BIBLIOGRAPHY

FEELINGS
-- Bloomfield, Harold H. M.D., with Felden, Leonard, Ph.D.
Making Peace With Yourself,
N.Y.: Ballantine Books, 1985

-- Gray, John, Ph.D. *What You Feel, You Can Heal*,
Mill Valley, Ca.: Heart Publishing, 1984

-- Helmstetter, Shad, Ph.D., *What To Say When You Talk To Yourself*
N.Y.: Pocket Books, 1987
_____, *Choices*
N.Y.: Pocket Books, 1989

-- Klagsbrun, Francine, *Mixed Feelings*
N.Y.: BantamBooks, 1992

-- McCarty, Meladee, and McCarty, Hanoch, *Acts of Kindness: How To Create a Kindness Revolution*
Deerfield Beach, Florida: Health Communications, Inc., 1994

-- Paul, Henry A., M.D., *When Kids Are Mad, Not Bad*
N.Y.: Berkley Books, 1995

-- Peter, Laurence, and Bill Dana, *The Laughter Prescription*
N.Y.: Ballantine Books, 1982

-- Rosellini, Gayle, and Worden, Mark*, Of Course, You're Anxious*
N.Y.: Harper Collins Publishers, 1991

-- Viscott, David, M.D., *Emotionally Free*
Chicago, Ill.: Contemporary Books, Inc., 1992

ANGER
-- Hankins, Gary, Ph.D. with Carol Hankins, *Prescription For Anger*
N.Y.: Warner Books, Inc., 1993

-- Larsen, Earnie, with Carol Larsen Hegarty, *From Anger To Forgiveness*
N.Y. : Ballantine Books, 1992

-- Lee, John, with Stott, Bill, *Facing The Fire*
N.Y. : Bantam Books, 1993

-- Luhn, Rebecca, R., Ph.D., *Managing Anger*
Los Altos, Ca. : Crisp Publications, Inc. 1992

-- McKay, Matthew, Ph.D., Rogers, Peter D., Ph.D., McKay, Judith, R.N. *When Anger Hurts*
Oakland, Ca. : New Harbinger Publications, Inc., 1989

-- Simon, Sidney B. and Simon, Suzanne, *Forgiveness - How To Make Peace With Your Past and Get On With Your Life*
N.Y.: Warner Books, Inc., 1991

-- Tavris, Carol, *Anger - The Misunderstood Emotion*
N.Y.: Simon and Schuster, 1989

-- Williams, Redford, M.D., and Williams, Virginia, Ph.D., *Anger Kills*
N.Y. : Harper Collins Publishers, Inc., 1993

DEPRESSION
-- Fontana, Vincent J. M.D., *Somewhere A Child Is Crying*
N.Y.: Macmillan Publishing Co. Inc., 1976

-- Giffin, Mary, M.D. and Felsenthal, Carol, *A Cry For Help*
Garden City, N.Y.: Doubleday and Co. Inc., 1983

-- Klagsbrun, Francine, *Too Young To Die*
N.Y.: PocketBooks, 1981

-- McCoy, Kathleen, Ph.D., *Understanding Your Teen Ager's Depression*
N.Y.: Berkley Publishing Group, 1994

-- Shapiro, Patricia Gottlieb, *A Parent's Guide To Childhood and Adolescent Depression*
N.Y.: DellPublishing, 1994

-- Shimberg, Elaine Fantle, *Depression: What Families Should Know*
N.Y.: Ballantine Books, 1993

PARENTING
-- Andersen, Eugene, et.al., *Self Esteem For Tots To Teens*
Deephaven, Mn. : Meadowbrook Publishers, 1984

-- Benson, Herbert, M.D., *The Relaxation Response*
N.Y.: Avon Books, 1976
_____, with Stark, Marg, *Timeless Healing*
N.Y. : Scribner, 1996

-- Berne, Pat and Savary, Lori, *Building Self-Esteem in Children*
N.Y. : Crossroad Publishing Co., 1985

-- Borba, Michele, Dr., *Esteem Builders*
Rolling Hills Estate, Ca. : Jamar Press, 1989

-- Borysenko, Joan, Ph.D. with Larry Rothstein, *Minding The Body, Mending The Mind*
N.Y.: Bantam Books, 1987

-- Briggs, Dorothy Corville, *Your Child's Self Esteem: The Key To Life*
N.Y. : Doubleday and Co. Inc., 1975

-- Canter, Lee with Canter, Marlene, *Assertive Discipline For Parents*
N.Y.: Harper and Row, 1988

-- Chopra, Deepak, M.D., *Creating Health*
Boston, Mass. : Houghton Mifflin Co., 1991

-- Clemes, Harris, and Bean, Reynold, *Self Esteem: The Key To Your Child's Well Being*
N.Y.: Zebra Books, 1982

-- Dyer, Wayne, *What Do You Really Want For Your Children?*
N.Y.: Avon Books, 1985

-- Elkind, David, *The Harried Child: Growing Up Too Fast Too Soon*
Reading, Ma.: Addison Wesley, 1981

-- Emery, Gary, Ph.D. and Campbell, James, M.D. *Rapid Relief From Emotional Distress*
N.Y.: Ballantine Books, 1986

-- Eyre, Linda and Eyre, Richard, *Teaching Children Responsibility*
N.Y.: Ballantine Books, 1991
_____, *Teaching Children Joy*
N.Y.: Ballantine Books, 1990
_____, *Teaching Your Child Values*
N.Y.: Simon and Schuster, 1993

-- Faber, Adele and Mazlish, Elaine, *Liberated Parents, Liberated Children*
N.Y.: Avon Books, 1974
_____, *How To Talk So Kids Will Listen and Listen So Kids Will Talk*
N.Y.: Avon Books, 1980

-- Ginott, Haim G. Dr., *Between Parent and Child*
N.Y.: Macmillan Publishing Co. Inc., 1965
_____, *Between Parent and Teenager*
N.Y.: Macmillan Publishing Co. Inc., 1969

-- Greene, Laurence J., *Smarter Kids*
N.Y. : Ballantine Books, 1987

-- Harris, James M., Ph.D., *You and Your Child's Self-Esteem*
N.Y.: Warner Books, Inc., 1989

-- Helmstetter, Shad, Ph.D., *Predictive Parenting*
N.Y.: Pocket Books, 1990

-- Knight, Michael E., *Teaching Children To Love Themselves: A Handbook For Parents and Teachers*
Englewood Cliffs, N.J.: Prentice - Hall, 1982

-- Kutner, Lawrence, Ph.D. *Parent and Child*
N.Y.: Avon Books, 1991

-- Lichona, Thomas, *Raising Good Children From Birth Through The Teenage Years*
N.Y.: Bantam Books, 1983

-- McKay, Matthew, and Tanning, Patrick, *Self Esteem*
N.Y. : St. Martin's Press, 1987

-- Nelsen, Jane, *Positive Discipline: Teaching Children Self-Discipline, Responsibility, Cooperation, and Problem-Solving Skills*
Fair Oaks, Ca. : Sunrise, 1981

-- Woititz, Janet G., Ed.D., *Healthy Parenting*
N.Y. : Simon and Schuster, 1992

-- Wright, H. Norman, *The Power of a Parent's Words*
Ventura, Ca.: Regal Books, 1991

-- Youngs, Bettie B., Ph.D. *Helping Your Teenager Deal With Stress*
Los Angeles, Ca. : Jeremy P. Tarcher, Inc., 1986

ABOUT THE AUTHOR

EDITH NAMM is both an Educator and a Specialized Handwriting Analyst. She holds a Master's Degree in Guidance from New York University and was certified as a Specialized Graphoanalyst by the Institute of Graphological Science in Dallas, Texas.

EDITH NAMM has 25 years of experience as a Guidance Counselor with the New York City Board of Education and in 1986 was honored as "The Outstanding Guidance Counselor" in District 21, Brooklyn. She has 10 years of experience as a Certified Specialized Graphonalyst and is a Member of the International Graphological Society.

EDITH is proud of her 42 years of experience as a Parent and is thoroughly enjoying her role as a Grandmother.